YES Chef!

Phillip McMillan

The ungarnished confessions of an Australian chef

FINCH PUBLISHING
SYDNEY

Yes Chef! The ungarnished confessions of an Australian chef

First published in 2012 in Australia and New Zealand by Finch Publishing Pty Limited,
ABN 49 057 285 248, Suite 2207, 4 Daydream Street, Warriewood, NSW, 2102, Australia.

13 12 8 7 6 5 4 3 2 1

National Library of Australia Cataloguing-in-Publication entry:

Mcmillan, Phillip.
Yes chef! : the ungarnished confessions of an Australian chef
/ Phillip McMillan.
9781921462818 (pbk.)
Mcmillan, Phillip--Childhood and youth. Cooks--Australia--Biography.
Cooking--Australia--History.Food--Australia--Anecdotes.
641.5092

Cover design by Creation Graphics
Edited by Megan Drinan
Editorial assistance by Karen Gee
Typeset in Adobe Garamond by Pier Vido
Printed by McPhersons Printing

**Ladies and gentlemen, the story you are about to hear is true.
Only the names have been changed.**

Contents

For Joanne, Aliesha and Tiarne

Chapter 1

Meat loaf and porcupine balls

How long does it take to cook cauliflower? Three minutes? Half an hour? Two and a half hours? The answer is not straightforward; it depends on who you ask. And it's a generational thing. How you cook vegetables says a lot about you: who you are, how old you are, even where you come from. It's a social and cultural barometer of sorts.

I cook cauliflower for about three or four minutes but I was brought up with it being cooked for two and half hours. I remember the vegetables being put on to cook at 3.30 pm after school. The vegetables were steamed for about half an hour then the pot was turned off. They were heated for another half an hour later on just before dinner. By the time they were served they needed surgical care to stop them from falling apart en route to the plate. They had also acquired a dull, yellowish colour and a stale cabbage smell.

Cooking the family meal was Mum's job. Dad's job was to mow the lawn, paint the house and sometimes cook on the barbeque outside. After work each night Dad would walk home from the railway station with two large bottles of Fosters lager under his arm. He would sit in the chair in the corner of the lounge room, drink the beer, watch the news on TV and wait for dinner to be served. I was expected to be home from roaming the neighborhood on my bike by about 6 pm. Dinner was then served. Often it was meat loaf, cauliflower, beans, mashed potato and Gravox gravy. Other nights it was sausages, beef rissoles, lamb forequarter chops or curried sausages, Heinz spaghetti in tomato sauce on white bread toast or Big Red tomato soup, savoury pancakes, potato pancakes or shepherd's pie.

'Camp Pie' also regularly graced our dinner table. Similar to spam, Camp Pie is a tinned corned beef product – food only in the loosest sense of the word. Mum would open the tin, cut into 1 cm slices and then fry in a pan. It had a grey, reddish brown appearance – a bit like Pal without the chunks and marrowbone jelly – and was probably similar to the contents of ration packs from the Second World War.

I grew up in Clayton, one of the then outer eastern suburbs of Melbourne. It was primarily a community of white Anglo-Saxons who worked hard, drove EH Holdens, dressed their kids in pressed shorts, checkered shirts and bow ties to go to Sunday school at the local Church of England and for whom the culinary highlight of the week was the Sunday roast.

Lunch was the preferred time for a Sunday roast. My brother and I would come home on our bikes from Sunday school, wash our hands and sit at the fully set table. We would say grace before eating – it was a formal occasion, after all – and when the meal was over, we had to ask formal permission to leave the table. The meat was usually lamb or chicken. Our family of five would eat one meal of roast chicken and still have enough left over for another whole family meal on Monday night. (How that was done I'm not really sure: if I have a roast chicken at home with my kids now, it serves four people with no leftovers.)

Dessert was mostly tinned fruit – pears, peaches or the exotic two fruits (pears and peaches) – with or without ice-cream. But on special occasions, we would have an apple pie or lemon delicious pudding made from lemons grown on the tree in corner of the backyard – the one the men of the family would urinate on. (They were convinced the acid was good for the lemons and I can't recall any harm coming of the practice!)

My father, Norm, worked as an electrical fitter repairing electrical systems in diesel trains, while my mother, Moira, was an Avon lady. My family history in Australia dates back to John McMillan, a twenty-two-year-old farming immigrant from Kintyre, Scotland. He arrived on the *Loch Rannoch* from Glasgow in December 1878 following four months at sea, probably having survived on a diet of salted meat and weevil-infested biscuits. The gold rush was over but he still travelled to Ballarat and became a farmer: the first in a long line of working class Australian

McMillan families. (The Scottish contribution to Australian culinary enlightenment seems to be limited to whisky, haggis and the deep fried Mars Bar. I am an ardent fan of Scotch whisky, but you can keep haggis and the deep fried Mars Bar!)

Mum and Dad never went to church but it was generally accepted that kids were christened and went to Sunday school to receive a basic religious education. It was all very important at the time. Prayers were said before going to sleep at night and ten cents was regularly placed in the church plate on Sunday. In reality, it was just a token effort, a show for society; what was expected of a white middle class family. I attended church but didn't really pay much attention. It all seemed a bit too restrictive for me. Apparently I was a sinner who needed redemption from God but for what I wasn't sure. Maybe it was for not eating all my vegetables.

Food was not a defining part of middle class life in my early years. It was, in general, quite boring, predictable, and of not much consequence. It was for nutrition, certainly not for entertainment or even enjoyment. The ultimate gourmet treat was to lick the bowl and beaters from a White Wings packet cake mix. (I could never understand why my mother bothered to bake the cake at all and swore that when I grew up I would make cake mixes for the batter only, but I never did.)

Our dinner menu hardly ever changed and food was rarely fussed over. It was dinner at home on all but a few occasions a year. To go out to a restaurant or pub for dinner was only ever contemplated for a very special occasion or while on a family holiday – we might have had dinner at the Rosebud pub on the Mornington Peninsula over the Christmas holidays, but that's about as extravagant as we would get. The only takeaway available was fish and chips with a sprinkle of vinegar. Later on, Kentucky Fried Chicken opened down the street. Dad was positive they used rabbit instead of chicken (he was under the impression that rabbit was much cheaper). Anyway, he said the rabbit was okay and the coleslaw was really good but it was very expensive compared to fish and chips. We might have had KFC once a year.

But the Clayton community was more diverse than it first appeared. Along with the Anglo-Saxons who inhabited the identical three-bedroom weatherboard houses, each with a well-manicured front lawn, an EH Holden parked in the drive and three kids roaming unsupervised, the Greeks and Italians also lived in Clayton. These New Australians were different to us: they ate different food and had a strange smell about them – a miasma of garlic, cheese, wine and tobacco. They had their own shops, too. Shops with a vast array of preserved meats hanging from ceiling hooks, lots of small jars full of everything from pickled cauliflower to anchovies. Then there was the range of at least fifty different cheeses, all of them smelling like old socks – not in Kraft blue and white packets on a shelf like ours, but big wheels of cheese in fridge displays that needed to be cut into smaller wedges when they were sold. The men would wear flat, European style caps and go to little shops with 'espresso' written on the window. They would sit there all day, smoking cigarettes, drinking coffee and playing cards. My father did none of this. It was very strange indeed. I figured it must be something sinister, maybe even the Mafia.

The Greeks had their own church, their own school after hours (Greek school) and their own food. They drove Valiants (which we called Greek Mercedes). The house next door to us was a rental property and sometimes newly arrived Greek families would live there for a few years before purchasing a new three-bedroom, brick-veneer home in a nearby street. Once in their own home, there seemed a great urgency to grow their own food. They would put every inch of dirt into food production, planting fruit trees and vegetable gardens everywhere, even in the front yard and on the nature strip. By our standards, this was rather crass compared to our neat lawn and picket fence. Our home had a big silver birch tree in the front yard and the backyard was a big lawn that was good for boys to play backyard cricket. Food production was limited to the famous lemon tree.

Like the Greeks, in our eyes, the Italians were different too. They were Catholic, and they would eat funny vegetables, drink that weird coffee that the Greeks liked and build big front gates with lion or eagle statues on each side of the driveway. They would plant grape vines and have a fig tree covered in a net next to a Roman fountain of a little boy pissing.

I could tell food was important to the Greeks and Italians. They pickled olives, made wine, cooked up vast batches of tomato sauce, used herbs like basil and oregano, marinated lamb, grilled squid and put garlic in everything. (My family made jam with quince from my grandparents' house or stewed fruit from the plum tree next door: it was the type of food that originated in the Depression out of necessity rather than a desire for quality and flavour.)

Our Greek neighbours would have huge family celebrations several times a year and especially at Easter. The whole scene was completely alien to us. They would build a big fire and spit roast a whole lamb in the backyard. My brother Gary and I would climb the fence, sit atop and watch. The Greeks would feed us lamb pieces straight off the spit while they drank wine, danced to *Zorba the Greek* and had a great time. We would never do such a thing. The Greeks smelt strange and spoke a different language, but their lamb was better than ours, much better.

Life is curious mix of fortune and misfortune; adventure and misadventure – and luck. One seemingly unrelated event can trigger a whole chain of events that you have no control over, cannot plan for, and at face value, seems to come out of nowhere.

When I was twelve years old, I had been working for a couple of years as a paperboy making a good $4 or $5 a week when one day, my brother Gary met with misfortune. No, he didn't die, but a wooden forklift pallet fell on his foot while he was working at the local fruit shop. The crushing of his toes was his pain, but my gain: realising that the fruit shop was now short staffed for about three weeks while Gary recovered. I lobbed up and applied for his job. To my amazement, the boss took me on and I went home to break the news to my brother and parents. It didn't go down well – I was a cheeky upstart seizing an opportunity at my brother's expense – but my parents had a meeting and I was allowed to keep the job.

I would ride my bike to the fruit shop after school and work from 4 pm to 6.30 pm each weekday as well as Saturday mornings, unloading the truck, cleaning the floors and sorting fruit. I worked hard and much to Gary's disgust I was offered a permanent job. As I toiled, I started to become more interested in food. I saw fruits and vegetables that I had never eaten before, food I never even knew existed. But these strange foods – eggplants, artichokes, capsicum, broccoli, olives, garlic, sweet potatoes, mangoes, prickly pear and chilli – were being bought by the Greeks and the Italians. Australians would buy carrots, peas, beans, potatoes and parsnips, but that's about all. After a while I had Italian mates and could swear and say all the numbers in Italian: an essential skill for a teenage boy.

Around this time I started a long association with alcohol. The lunchroom always had a fridge full of beer and, despite my age, I was allowed to knock off a drink or two on a Saturday. This was also the day the guy from the local bottle shop would come in for the boss's weekly booze order. Copious amounts of alcohol were ordered every week – beer, brandy, Cointreau, Bailey's Irish Cream, the lot. But he wasn't a drunk, he was just a great guy who liked beer, the Carlton football club and business.

When the boss's order had been taken, the bottle shop guy would ask all the staff for their order. One day, Gary, who had returned to work, ordered half a dozen cans of Melbourne Bitter. The bottle shop guy then looked at me and pointed his finger. 'Half a dozen cans of Melbourne,' I sheepishly replied. 'Okay,' he said. An hour later, the beer was delivered and I paid him about $2; an hour's pay. I was the proud owner of six cans of beer.

It wasn't long before my Italian mate and I were ordering half-size bottles of Johnny Walker Black Label for $5. We would hide the whisky at the back of the shop and pick it up after ice-skating on a Saturday night. Pizza, pinball and whisky poured into our cans of coke. It all seemed a natural thing to do – Dad had a beer every day and it seemed to make him happy, so why not me?

Then one day, when I was about fifteen, I was working with the boss's wife, Mrs Nan. We were cleaning and tidying the shop and I was telling her how I would buy some of these strange vegetables, take them home and cook them out of curiosity, following the second-hand recipes gathered from customers and my workmate Stephen.

'You should be a chef!' she said. Before this, the thought had never occurred to me. Mrs Nan explained that a chef was a highly respectable career and paid very well. It turned out she was wrong on both counts, but the thought gained traction in my impressionable mind.

My interest in good food kept growing. In fact, by 1981 I spent much of year twelve at the Caulfield Institute swapping recipes and cooking tips with my chemistry teacher Steve Murphy at the Racecourse Hotel on my lunch break. Then, when I was seventeen, going on holidays with your parents is the last thing you want to do, so my parents left me at home while they went to Queensland with my younger sister. I decided I wanted to have a real dinner party and cook a three-course meal for all my friends. It was 9 May 1981 and my life was about to change again.

I developed a menu and invited friends. We had chicken and sweetcorn soup for a starter, and beef and rice meatballs cooked in tomato soup known as porcupine balls for main course (a recipe straight out of a *Women's Weekly* cookbook). The meatballs were accompanied by sliced potato cooked with lemon juice and black pepper, honeyed carrots and beans with bacon. Dessert was apple strudel and ice-cream.

Somehow we all stayed sober and the food was good. After the main course I did lose a little interest in what I was doing because of the presence of a girl, Joanne. Another friend had invited her but I seemed to grab her attention more than he did. She had long dark hair and big green eyes; she looked more Italian or Spanish than her name Macdonald suggested. I had no idea that she actually liked me – I could never have picked up a girl like that if I was trying, the cards just fell my way that night.

I invited her back a few days later for lunch and cooked some veal schnitzel. We started to date and we were married in 1985. Twenty-seven years and two daughters later the bonds are still strong – and yes, we still eat the porcupine balls as a family meal.

When Joanne and I started going out we were young with a life of promise ahead of us but no real direction. At school I didn't have to try very hard to pass all my subjects. Most of my mates went on to university and became engineers of some sort, but I didn't want to delay getting into the big wide world by another four or five years at school. I was in a hurry: a big hurry. But for what I don't know. I just knew that I needed to work and cooking sounded as good as anything else – despite the fact that I had no idea what the job actually entailed.

In 1981 I was young, naive and totally unrealistic. Teenagers now are much better informed and much more opinionated than I ever was. The cult of the celebrity was not around like it is now: there was no internet, no mobile phones, no pay TV and no Facebook. Only famous people were famous and you had to do something real to be famous, like invent penicillin, kick a hundred goals or be prime minister. Over the last couple of years, even chefs have started to become cool. For me, it was not the celebrity image of a chef that led me to cooking; it was just something to do.

Chapter 2

'Yes, chef!'

The road to becoming a chef starts off very slowly and is really not very stimulating at all. It's a very structured training environment; there is a lot to learn and you are not let near the stove for quite a while. I spent the first year peeling carrots, trimming beans, makes crepes and various other simple dessert and cold dishes, working in the section of the kitchen called the larder. When I finally did get into TAFE in my second year, it was at the newly opened Box Hill College of TAFE where the facilities we great: there were shiny new kitchens, theatre-style classrooms and a training restaurant.

Most of the teachers were old German and Swiss chefs left over from the Olympics, the Southern Cross Hotel or the Hilton Hotel (the main two international hotels in Melbourne from the old days). Our first year chef was, however, not German or Swiss – he was a portly Australian chef with a moustache, and a rough, gravelly voice. He wasn't there to make friends; he was there to do a job. Chef William was in fact a very nice guy, but in the kitchen or classroom it was all business to him.

The first rule we learnt was that his name was 'chef' and when given instructions, we were to reply with, 'Yes, chef!'. The second rule was the uniform. It was to be black and white check pants (small squares only), white, starched, long-sleeve chef's jacket with white buttons (no black trimming), white clogs or black leather shoes, white neckerchief neatly tied with a half Windsor knot in the middle hanging down. In the kitchen we also wore a white, starched, chef's hat with pleats all around, not too tall so as to be as high as Chef Willliam's but tall enough to stand up and look impressive. Thirdly, if the uniform is not perfect, don't bother turning up to class. Forgot your neckerchief? Tough luck. You couldn't even attend the theory classes in the classrooms, you would have to go out to a local uniform store and buy one and then return to school late. And finally, the fourth rule: never enter a class late. Always sit in the canteen and wait for the next class. The same went for assignments: ten per cent off for every day late, even on weekends. Five days late and you have lost fifty per cent of your marks before you even start. In essence, they ran it like a military academy with the guns replaced by knives.

The first class was all about knife skills and vegetables cuts: julienne, brunoise, jardinière, paysanne, macedoine and mirepoix. Luckily I managed to get through the class without cutting myself thanks to the year's experience I'd already had. Knife skills were followed by basic classes on chopping parsley and lemon slices, peeling tomatoes, making tomato concassé, cutting potatoes in one hundred and one different ways, filleting fish, crumbing schnitzels and trimming meat – all the basics before we really started to cook in the second year.

In my second year, we methodically worked through the principles of cookery with Chef Norbert, the Swiss executive sous chef from the Hilton who drove the bus for the Church of Christ on weekends. It was boiling the first week, followed by steaming, poaching, shallow frying, deep frying, baking, roasting, stewing, grilling and braising. This was quickly followed by soups, sauces, pastry and desserts: a passing parade of classical dishes straight out of *Hering's*; none of which could be put on a modern menu.

Modern menus are very different in style and content. Dishes are much more creative and make use of many more ingredients than were ever available to chefs in the formation of classical European cooking. Most menus now use a description of the ingredients and cooking methods because there is no classical name for the dishes that are on most menus today. It might be a creation of that particular chef or a modern dish created by another chef. For example, masala-spiced blue eye, pan-fried and served with seared tomato, sautéed spinach, curry oil and date chutney.

In our third year we traded the Swiss sous chef for a tall German chef named Chef Eberhard and cooked in the school restaurant known as Fountains. Each week one student would be the head chef while we rotated through the other positions. The menu was a little bit more modern but was still ninety per cent classical.

Apart from the kitchen practical, we had classes in kitchen theory, nutrition, business and history. Kitchen theory included learning the different slow cooking methods for tough cuts of meat such as stewing (small cubes of meat simmered fully submerged in a pot on top on the stove) and braising (meat cooked in a pan in the oven as a large joint, half covered with liquid and a lid over the pan).

As well as all this technical stuff that explained what cooking actually was, we also learnt about history and the development of the modern kitchen. Most importantly, we learnt about the kitchen brigade: a very formal hierarchy of cooks and chefs according to long-established titles and traditions.

Auguste Escoffier (1846–1935) introduced the brigade system. A chef, writer, business manager and an innovative thinker, Escoffier is considered the father of the modern French kitchen. He transformed the French haute cuisine he inherited from chefs such as Marie-Antoine Carême (1784–1833), modernised the style and added a lot more structure.

Understanding the brigade system helps explain the role of a chef; the day-to-day life of many cooks and chefs throughout the world; the situation I was in; and the bigger system I was a part of whether I liked it or not. We came to understand that we were all at the bottom of this ladder: there was a long road ahead before we could stop cleaning beans and slicing potatoes.

The kitchen steward or kitchen hand (sometimes known as the dish pig) is probably what was originally known as a plongeur (dishwasher) or garçon de cuisine (kitchen boy). Chefs are messy bastards because they always have somebody else to clean up after them – and that person is the dish pig. It might sound harsh to call a fellow worker a pig, but I assure you it is a term of endearment: the dish pig is a highly valued and respected part of the brigade.

A good dish pig is someone who turns up every day for work and can handle the shouting and chaos that is a commercial kitchen. Someone who can really get the work done without sinking into a pool of self pity or envy of others. He understands that this is where he is at in life at the moment and makes the best of it; he is an optimist. (I say 'he' because most dish pigs are male.) On the upside, he can have almost anything he wants within reason. He is always well fed as the chefs know they rely on him: he wants fish for dinner? Okay. He wants to drink the leftover half bottles of wine? Okay. He wants you to place the used pans in a particular place? Okay.

During service a cook will use a lot of pans – more pans than they actually have – so they will need to be washed, dried and placed back in the pile for the cook to use again. The pans are usually all steel with steel handles so they can cook on the stove and in the oven and they may come straight into the wash area within a minute or two of being used. A dish pig knows from bitter experience to *never* pick up a pan with their hands; always use a dry cloth. So, if a cook treats a dish pig badly, he may find a red-hot pan cleaned in thirty seconds and placed back on the top of the pile ready for him to pick up and burn his hand during service. Alternatively, he may simply find his pans are not getting washed at all, ruining the cook's momentum and service all together. Treat him well and he will help by peeling some onions, fetching you more cream and not telling the chef that you're looking for another job.

An apprentice is the first step to becoming a real chef. In the beginning, an apprentice may start with very boring jobs like peeling potatoes, cleaning beans and endless cutting (often of their own hands). There is no time off for an injury, so patch it up, put on a glove and get back to work. But as an apprentice gains more experience, they are let loose on cooking the food. They might start on the fry station and the cold section and then progress onto the hot sections. But stuff up and you will be making Caesar salad and potato wedges with sour cream for the rest of your sentence.

When an apprentice has finally finished the four years of indentured slavery that is their apprenticeship, they progress to becoming a commis. The commis's role is production and service and it's great no longer being at the bottom of the ladder. At this stage you know how to cook, but others in the kitchen are still a lot better and more experienced than you. A commis works for, reports to and is the bitch of the chef de partie. The section the commis works in also determines their rank: a commis in the saucier (sauces) is higher ranking than a commis in the entremetier (vegetables) who is in turn higher than a commis in the garde manger (cold section).

A demi-chef position is like an encouragement award for the commis. It shows that you are on your way to becoming a chef de partie with your own small party of slaves to follow your instructions. Keep working hard, never take a day off, keep up with the dockets during service, don't waste food, work extra hours for free, don't complain and answer every question from those above you with, 'Yes, chef!' and one day you will become a chef de partie.

The chef de partie is the chef in charge of one section of the kitchen (a large brigade may have about six sections). A chef de partie reports to the sous chef and the chef de cuisine. Different sections include the following:

- The saucier is ranked the highest and most prestigious of all the sections. They are responsible for making sauces, finishing meat dishes and may cook fish dishes for service.
- The rotisseur, or the roast section, is often combined with the saucier in smaller kitchens. The rotisseur also contains the grillardin (grill cook) and the friturier (fry cook).
- The entremetier handles soups, hot entrées, vegetables and egg dishes.

- The garde manger handles the cold kitchen, salads, cold dishes, cold buffet platters and some basic preparations such as lemon wedges, herb garnishes etc.
- The pâtissier, or pastry cook and bakers make the desserts, breads and cakes. In a large venue the patisserie is a separate kitchen with its own staff and kingdom. Stay in good with the pâtissier; he always has good alcohol to drink and croissants to eat. Make a friend of him and you start every day with Danish pastries straight from the oven, a shot of Irish whiskey and a kind word. Locked in the dungeons of the hotel starting at 4 am, he is happy just for the company.
- The butcher usually has a separate section in a separate kitchen; they don't usually associate with chefs that much.

The chef de tournant is usually at the chef de partie level and is considered a high-level position. The tournant is the hired gun of the kitchen and can work in all sections; they might fill in on days off while others are on holidays or when a section needs extra help.

The term friturier (fry chef) is not really used much in Australia but the other terms are still in common use.

Meaning 'under chef' in French, the sous chef is second in charge of the kitchen and reports to the chef de cuisine. The sous chef is typically doing a lot of ordering of supplies, management of staff, rosters and often works the 'pass' (that is plating and inspecting food as it is served by the cooks). In the absence of the chef de cuisine the sous chef has full authority. Becoming a sous chef is a big deal as you get a jacket with your name printed on it and get to wear black pants instead of check pants. For the first time in your career you actually look like a chef!

The chef de cuisine is the chef in charge of the kitchen. They report to the executive sous chef and the executive chef and have full management authority and responsibility for all staff issues, menu development, purchasing of ingredients, recipes and all financial outcomes (food cost percentage, wages cost). If a hotel has five restaurants, each restaurant will have its own chef de cuisine and at least one sous chef in each.

An executive sous chef is second in charge of the whole hotel or venue. They may have five or more food outlets to supervise and will help a chef de cuisine with any problems they have. An exec sous will spend most of their time in the outlet that gives them the most problems. It is best if they don't hang around too much as they feel they should help with the cooking but have lost the speed and agility of the younger cooks. They are usually on the hunt for a promotion to executive chef and will cut anybody down to get it.

The executive chef is the general, a living god. They have absolute control and power over all things food. They are always impeccably groomed, well spoken and usually highly intelligent. Like the exec sous chef, they don't really do any cooking as they are now a full-time manager looking at budgets, menus, concepts, forward plans and handling all the other management teams such as the food and beverage manager and the general manager.

A kitchen is not a democracy. It is a military dictatorship where absolute obedience is demanded – and received. Anybody above you in the hierarchy is called, 'chef'. To call a chef anything else is unthinkable; it is a mark of respect. Even a general manager will call a chef de cuisine, 'chef'. The chef is the total dictator of the kitchen. Anybody, and I mean anybody else who enters the kitchen is now in the chef's domain. Every piece of food in the kitchen belongs to the chef, every cook or dish pig in the kitchen belongs to the chef. If a waiter, manager or even the restaurant owner wants something to eat they ask the chef – and they do so in a polite manner.

A kitchen is no place for a generation of consensus orientated, politically correct vegan civil rights activists, no place for crying girls, or boys for that matter, and no place for clock watchers: they can all rack off out of a professional kitchen.

I came out of TAFE a much more rounded, confident cook with a better understanding of the actual job of a chef. I realised that cooking is a vocation that takes over your whole life and is all consuming. It is not a job where you rock up an hour before the restaurant opens and have a think about what you might cook for dinner that night. Much of the job involves decision making around menus, keeping the food preparation under control, coping with staff and above all, making a profit.

Imagine a typical Saturday night in a chef's life. It's around 6.30 pm and you are about to start serving between one hundred and one hundred and fifty people, or covers, from an à la carte menu. As each guest is seated the waiter might give them a little freebie taste, or what is known as an 'amose bouche'. Apart from coming up with a new and fresh idea every day for the amose bouche, this is really not too much of a problem as by now these should have been prepared so that the waiter can just serve them to the guests without too much extra effort on your part.

The menu has a choice of eight entrées, twelve main courses and seven desserts. Each dish may have up to seven components. For example 'Seared Four Peppercorn Salmon with Citrus and Melon Relish and Mixed Grain Pilaf' sounds simple but count the components:

1) trimmed and portioned salmon
2) four peppercorn mix
3) citrus and melon relish
4) pilaf of mixed grain (rice, wild rice, cous cous)
5) parsley oil for colour and flavour
6) julienne of red cabbage, carrot, spring onion, cabbage
7) lemon halves that have been seared with sugar and grilled
8) a slow baked garnish of crispy salmon skin.

So how many salmon do you think you will sell? How many did you sell last night? How many did you sell last Saturday? What are bookings like for Sunday? If you prepare too many portions will they all be sold on Sunday or will they hang around in the fridge till Monday or Tuesday?

Multiply this by twelve different main courses, plus the two special dishes also being offered, and you are starting to get an idea of what the daunting task of the 'mis en place' is (mis en place is the French term for preparation, to have everything ready and in place). Then do it again for the eight entrees and the seven desserts. Out of one hundred and fifty covers, how many will order an entrée? How many will order a dessert? You would think that with records of past sales you should be able to work all this out without too much bother. Well, yes and no. You do have the statistics from the point of sale (POS) system but every day is different. Last week it was raining and this week it's much warmer, George made a great pork belly dish last night on *MasterChef* and today everybody decides to order the pork belly. Anything can happen and often does.

You see a chef has to not only make all these decisions, prepare all the food, cook all the food, serve all the food, he also has to *make a profit.* Yes, that's right my friends, a big part of a chef's job is to make a profit. Each portion of fish that is not sold and thrown out will cost anywhere upwards of $7. Each of those lovely crispy salmon skin garnishes may not cost a lot in actual ingredients, but to get them just the right shape and texture requires the time and careful attention of a skilled cook which you will pay for.

A chef is also a personnel manager and responsible for the actions of their staff, as well as the hiring and firing of the whole team. If the cook went out last night, got drunk and became very close friends with the new waitress, it's your problem that he is now working at half pace and playing cutesy eyes with her in the hope of a repeat performance tonight, if he can get the desserts out quick enough.

The kicker is that the customers do not really give a stuff about any problems behind the scenes. They make a booking, have high expectations and pay good money. Your wife/husband/partner is pissed off with you because you missed their birthday again! Nobody cares! Your knees are killing you from years of bending down to the oven. Nobody cares! The fish supplier was an hour and a half late so you didn't have time to prepare all the seafood. Nobody cares! Your arse has a strange rash (known in the trade as chefs' arse) and the only thing that seems to give relief is a liberal coating of cornflour. Nobody cares! One of the underbench fridges has broken down. Nobody cares! The apprentice overcooked the potatoes. Nobody cares!

A chef's life is all about getting the job done, and after TAFE I understood what I was getting myself in for. I now had all the tools to make a career, but what sort of career did I want?

Chapter 3

The eighties

In the seventies and eighties, most people simply couldn't afford dining at a restaurant very often and their taste in food didn't extend much beyond chops and three veg or a carvery buffet anyway.

One of the few occasions my family did go to a restaurant was when I was about fifteen or sixteen years old. It was my parents' twenty-fifth wedding anniversary and it would have been about 1978. I'm not sure where my sister was but my girlfriend and I, my older brother and his girlfriend all went to the Swagman Restaurant in Ferntree Gully with my parents.

The Swagman was famous for a number of reasons: it was really big (seating about 1200 covers); it had a huge floor show of singers and dancers; and it was constantly advertising on television. The Swagman was a smorgasbord restaurant and I remember my father piling on the prawns, salads, cold cuts and roast meats: there was every conceivable type of bulk cheap food you could think of. It wasn't pretty, but you could eat as much as you wanted and be entertained along the way. The floor-show host would call out all the birthdays, wedding anniversaries, special occasions and celebrations. It was pretty corny, but very popular at the time.

Another popular restaurant of the era was the Cuckoo in the Dandenongs. One of the first restaurants in Melbourne, it opened in the late fifties and was hosted by German Chef Willi Koeppen and his wife Karin. With the TV show, *The Chef Presents* in 1957, Willi really was one of the first celebrity chefs. It was one of many smorgasbord-type restaurants of the era with a Bavarian theme, complete with oompah band, leather lederhosen and thigh-slapping dancing. Mysteriously, one day in 1976 Willi went for a walk and was never seen or heard from again. Despite the changes in hospitality, restaurants and also in people's taste in the past fifty years, the Cuckoo is still going strong today – mainly due to buses of tourists eager for the 'authentic' Australian experience of a traditional Bavarian restaurant including grown men in leather shorts within an Australian rainforest setting.

Another restaurant, Alexander's, on the corner of the Nepean Highway and North Road Gardenvale, was a big smorgasbord restaurant seating about four hundred covers with a Glenn Miller big band theme. A mate of mine, Martin, worked there and they would get pumped every night; *enormous* food production. Cheap and simple but all you could eat with a big band and dancing.

Anyone born after about 1980 wouldn't be familiar with the scene, but family wallets weren't too fat back then: people just didn't go out to a restaurant for the sake of it – it had to be a special occasion. So restaurants had floor shows, themes, bands and dance floors. It was a big deal: birthday cakes, uncles, aunties, singing and dancing, everyone had a good time. The food in general was fairly simple, but there was a lot of it – a man was expected to gorge himself, especially at a smorgasbord restaurant.

The Bavarian smorgasbords were food for the suburban middle class masses (my family was squarely in this category). But when I think about it, there were also some really good restaurants and some really good chefs. But these were out of the league of most people other than wealthy business types in the CBD and those of fresh European origin who actually knew what good food was. I certainly never went to any of them.

Hospitality professionals and good chefs ran these well-known, upmarket restaurants. The food was not like it is today; it was very classical and very European. Restaurants like Two Faces run by Swiss Chef Hermann Schneider, Fanny's and Glo Glo's run by Gloria Staley, Vlado's the famous steak restaurant in Richmond, Jimmy Watson's Wine Bar in Carlton, Petty Sessions run by Richard Frank, Stephanie's by Stephanie Alexander and Mietta's in various forms run by Mietta O'Donnell produced classically French food of a very high standard.

It was in this era that I started cooking in 1982 at a restaurant in Beaumaris called the Didgeridoo. The Didge was also one of the early pioneer restaurants of the sixties and seventies and in its day was a big attraction and a very popular restaurant. The interior of the restaurant was decorated like a cave with moulded fibreglass walls and a dark atmosphere. By the time I started working there as an apprentice, however, it was on the decline: food was served on dented stainless steel oval platters, stainless steel coupes and chipped white 10-inch plates. (In fact, it was to last only another six months before going broke and being demolished.)

The Didge was owned by an old German woman, Mrs Bierman, whom, like the restaurant, was not much longer for this earth, but this I could recognise, or at least smell, when each morning I had to knock on the door of her adjoining flat to pick up the keys. An old woman just out of bed; no young man should experience what I saw.

The barman and gofer around the place, Anton, was about fifty-five and also German. The chef, Ulrich was, as you would also expect, German. He was about forty-five years old and would entertain us with stories of working as a mercenary in the Belgian Congo during the seventies that included shooting an Uzi, throwing grenades into the river to catch fish and blowing up trucks. With scars all over his body, he was easy to believe.

It was my job to go to Anton every day and get a large glass of spirit or liqueur for the chef. It would be whisky one day, cognanc the next, sometimes Galliano or even a sambuca. The usual excuse was that it was for the chocolate mousse, but the reality was the chef liked a drink. His moods were unpredictable; nasty one minute then all kindness the next. One moment he would take the time to show me something new; the next he would humiliate me by giving me a task well beyond my capabilities and watch me fail.

One of the cruelest things he would do was make me cook staff meals. I was eighteen and really had no idea how to cook. Once, I didn't know how to crumb a schnitzel, so I didn't use flour. The egg didn't stick to the meat and then the crumbs didn't stick, either. The meal was terrible. I knew it and so did everybody else. The worst thing was, he had watched me cook the whole thing, but didn't say anything until he finally humiliated me in front of everybody by calling the meal shit.

That's just the way it was though; many old chefs treated apprentices badly in the belief that they were toughening them up and preparing them for the job of a chef. Those that could not hack it would never survive as a chef anyway; so either way they were convinced they were right.

My introduction to cooking had been bittersweet, but it was a start. After three months though, the time had come to sign my apprentice papers and contract me to the restaurant. Ulrich said to be quick and get out while I could, as if I signed the papers I would sink with the ship: it might be a slow death or a fast death but death was assured. He arranged an interview for me with the Cordon Bleu staffing agency.

Within about a week, I had a new job at a restaurant in Ringwood called The High Street Tavern.

The Tavern seated about 120 covers; it was full on Fridays and Saturdays and did a brisk business other nights. Lunches were quiet, but we needed time for prep anyway. It was owned by a husband and wife team, Bart and Bev – he was a Swiss chef and she was an extrovert restaurateur. It was a family-type environment.

Owner chefs are intense; very intense. Everything has to be done just so: every carrot, every salad dressing, every crepe, every onion ring and every parsley stalk. They are very stifling conditions to work under every day. But on the upside, Bart really taught me classical cooking using traditional methods. And as I know now, most owner chefs prefer fresh clay – the unadulterated mind of a young apprentice that can be moulded in their own image. Meanwhile, Bev methodically introduced me to French wine; the German waitress, Elise, and I would drink all the leftover wine from lunch every day; and Bart and I would start a busy service with a shot of brandy. Just the right environment for a seasoned drinker like me.

Bart and Bev also had another outlet, a simpler bistro operation a few doors up. Joanne would waitress there on a Saturday night while I pumped out one hundred and twenty à la carte at the Tavern. After the customers had gone we would all sit around drinking wine and eating pâté. Barmen and chefs from the whole area would call in every week to drink more and talk industry talk. In September 1983 we set up a TV and watched the America's Cup until the early morning hours and we played Men at Work's *Down under*, over and over on the PA in the restaurant.

I stayed at the Tavern for the whole of my apprenticeship. These were simple but good times: learning to cook and drink wine; tapas-style snacks all night; seeing a whole side of life that I had never seen growing up. Joanne and I soaked up the whole thing – we loved working in hospitality. Bart and Bev were mentors to us – we wanted to be just like them.

The restaurant and hotel scene from the fifties to the early eighties had been dominated by the Germans and the Swiss. The Italians were establishing Lygon Street and restaurants like Pellegrino's and the Chinese, of course, had Chinatown and restaurants in the suburbs with their own staff and chefs, but the Germans and the Swiss were the leading chefs in Australia and even in most parts of the world at the time. Almost all executive chefs and executive sous chefs at the international hotels were German or Swiss. They were great at organising and managing so were well suited to hotels in particular. Many of these chefs arrived for or around the time of the 1956 Olympics in Melbourne: they came, they cooked and they stayed. Many of the chefs at TAFE (culinary school) when I was an apprentice were also older German and Swiss chefs and most had excellent experience with the Hilton, Intercontinental or other international hotel chains.

When I started TAFE, the German and Swiss cooking teachers told me to buy three books: *Practical professional cookery* by Cracknell and Kaufmann; *Larousse gastronomique*, the classical French book and *Hering's Dictionary of classical and modern cookery*.

Cracknell and Kauffman, or C and K as it was known, was the standard book for apprentices at the time. It had all the recipes you needed. First published in 1972, it was in use throughout the English-speaking world. *Larousse gastronomique*, first published in 1938, is a classical book of French cuisine. Hering's is interesting: it is not a recipe book, instead, it is a dictionary of classical dishes and lists the ingredients in each dish. First published by Richard Hering in 1907, it was translated into English by Walter Bickel.

Almost all the dishes served in the early eighties were classical European dishes: there was little or no innovation. Each dish had a name in French, often places, regions or ingredients, but sometimes the chef named the dish in honour of famous people. For example, in the late 1800s, French chef Auguste Escoffier invented the Peach Melba after the Australian soprano, Dame Nellie Melba. Menus used the classical names with or without a description. It was tournedos Rossini, chicken Kiev, Wiener schnitzel, steak diane, coquilles St Jacques, flounder véronique, lobster thermidor and crepe suzette. Other common French terms used include the following:

à l'anglaise – English style (ie boiled)

à la hongroise – Hungarian style (ie paprika)

à la russe – Russian style

à la lyonnaise – with onions

à la bordelaise – with red wine

à la florentine – with spinach

When I was as an apprentice, the standard dishes in most restaurants were porterhouse maître d'hôtel (a porterhouse steak with parsley butter), garlic prawns in a béchamel and cream sauce on rice, seafood cocktails, prawn cocktails and chicken and mushroom crepes topped with hollandaise sauce.

Avocado salad and seafood avocado were also popular entrées at the time. To make an avocado salad, half an avocado was peeled and sliced, fanned on a plate with iceberg lettuce, tomato, black olives, alfalfa and French dressing. Seafood avocado comprised pieces of fish, scallops and small shrimp bound together in a cocktail sauce and placed on half an avocado. Add iceberg lettuce, alfalfa, a black olive, a sprinkle paprika and chopped parsley and you have yourself an entrée.

Another common entrée of the time was pâté maison (meaning house pâté), made from chicken livers. We actually made quite a nice pâté maison using lots of bacon fat, butter and fresh herbs to give a nice rich flavor. But the presentation will give you a good idea of the times. Once the pâté had been cooked it was puréed in a food processor and rolled in aluminum foil. To serve, we would remove some foil, slice into three discs and place on a plate of iceberg lettuce, add garnishes of onion rings, toast triangles, black olives, alfalfa and finally a parsley sprig. *Every dish was garnished with parsley.* So much so that by the nineties, no respectable chef would use parsley as a garnish. To do so would show that you were living in the past; cooking in the past. Except, of course, unless you were one of those old Swiss or German chefs still making Russian salad, eggs mayonnaise and schnitzel Holstein.

Every restaurant had oysters natural and kilpatrick on every entrée menu, it was just expected. Kilpatrick oysters are oysters topped with bacon and Worcestershire sauce then grilled under the salamander (overhead grill) until the bacon is crispy. Served on a stainless steel round plate on a bed of rock salt, it was garnished with lemon and, of course, a parsley sprig. Adventurous chefs would also place oysters mornay or oysters florentine on the menu; both would use a heavy béchamel sauce, mornay with cheese and Florentine with spinach.

Seafood cocktails were also a standard on every menu. Served in stainless steel coupes, a nice leaf of iceberg lettuce was topped with a little chiffonade of iceberg (shredded iceberg) and some poached mixed seafood in cocktail sauce. Garnished with a slice of boiled egg, some chopped parsley and a lemon wedge, the whole thing was then dusted with paprika. Voilà, one of the most popular entrées ever.

Smoked salmon was an entrée on most menus. It was generally imported from Denmark, but the really good stuff was from Scotland. It was served on a plate with iceberg lettuce, onion rings, capers and horseradish cream with toast on the side. Now we have a ready supply of farmed salmon from Tasmania, smoked salmon is very common and not very special any more. You would expect more of a chef than to place pre-sliced smoked salmon on a plate with toast and onion rings, but at the time, it was a really special treat.

Soups were pumpkin (known in the trade as the restaurateurs friend because of the good profit margin), French onion, minestrone, leek and potato, and pea and ham – all standard European fare served with bread croutons (sippets) and sprinkled with chopped parsley.

Main courses were likewise very traditional. Most fish dishes were served with a meunière sauce of butter, chopped parsley and lemon. Sometimes capers would be added if we wanted to be adventurous but Australians didn't really know what capers were and often didn't like the sharp flavour. Garnishes included lemon slices dipped in chopped parsley or paprika, van dyke lemons (cut into a zigzag pattern) and a parsley sprig, or maybe a sprig of dill if we wanted to be different. When I first started cooking, fresh Tasmanian Atlantic salmon wasn't available. It wasn't until about 1985 or 1986 that we started to get Tasmanian salmon, both fresh and smoked; it's common now but back then it was exotic.

Porterhouse maître d'hôtel and steak au poivre (pepper steak) were the most popular dishes by far. Maître d'hôtel is a very nice butter flavoured with parsley and lemon juice. The pepper steak would be dusted with cracked pepper and for the sauce, we would use a demi-glace base with green peppercorns from a bottle. The interesting question is, why were steaks so popular? It may have been that the average person never really knew how to cook a steak or where to get a good quality steak from so it was considered a luxury to have one cooked by a professional chef with a tasty sauce or flavoured butter.

Homemade pies were also popular. Steak and kidney was the most popular, made by stewing the steak and kidney, heating in a ramekin bowl, placing puff pastry over the top and baking until the pastry was cooked. Beef Wellington was another favorite: fillet steaks were topped with duxelles (chopped mushrooms sautéed in a herb butter) and pâté then wrapped in puff pastry and baked. Individual serves could be pre-prepared and cooked to order.

Classical dishes such as duck aux cerises (duck with cherries) and duck a l'orange (duck with orange) were standards on many menus. Ducks were roasted, cooled and portioned into two halves with the main rib cage removed. On ordering, the half duck would be placed in the oven with some chicken stock to be heated through and when ready, the stock was poured off and replaced with a hot, ready-made sauce. The duck was served simply coated with the sauce and garnished with parsley.

Lamb was usually a rack of lamb. Usually four ribs were trimmed (not as well as they would be now) with often a thick layer of fat left on the top. The bottom bone would even be left in in some restaurants and a little mashed potato was used to hold the rack in place on the plate.

Mint or honey sauces were standard and the lamb was garnished with a rosemary or parsley sprig.

Veal was always called veal scallopini regardless of whether it was served with a mushroom, lemon or madeira sauce. Thin slices of veal were sautéed and the sauce (always finished with cream to give it a smoothness and richness) was finished in the pan for extra flavour. The sauce was garnished with a parsley sprig and it was ready.

There weren't many classical ways to serve pork other than roast pork but we often used pork fillets with various fillings (apples and prunes were a favourite) down the centre, served with a cranberry demi-glace sauce. The exceptions were some German dishes, such as kassler, where smoked pork loin was heated with white wine and sauerkraut and served with mashed potato.

Prawns were always garlic prawns or curried prawns served on a bed of rice. Chicken was usually fillets stuffed with various fillings such as seafood with a champagne sauce, spinach and pine nuts, apricot or mango (with a chicken mousse base and a white wine cream sauce) or duxelles (mushroom with a cream demi-glace sauce). We did also serve classical dishes such as coq au vin and ballotine of chicken (the bone removed from the leg and thigh and the cavity filled with a pork mousse and served with a cranberry demi-glace sauce). Sometimes, though, it was also as simple as chicken provençale (half a roasted chicken with a demi-glace sauce garnished with capsicum, tomato, parsley and olives).

All meals were served with potatoes and two vegetables. Pommes boulangère was the most common (sliced potatoes cooked in a tray with onions, butter and chicken stock) but pommes dauphinoise (cooked with onion, garlic, milk or cream and cheese) was also popular. So were pommes croquettes, pommes william (mashed potato moulded into the shape of a pear and crumbed then deep fried) and pommes duchesse (mashed potato piped into a tower shape and then baked).

Vegetables were often glazed carrots in sugar, honey or orange juice finished with butter and chopped parsley; green beans with bacon and onion; cauliflower mornay or polonaise (finely chopped hard-boiled eggs and breadcrumbs), braised red cabbage with apple, cloves and cinnamon, brussels sprouts with bacon or zucchini with napoli sauce.

Side dishes did not exist in the eighties as customers expected a full meal for the price. It wasn't until the nineties that restaurateurs discovered that people would pay extra for vegetables if you make the main course small enough, and there was a subtle but real change going on in restaurants all over Melbourne in that chefs wanted a style of cooking that enabled cauliflower to taste like cauliflower and carrots to taste like carrots. It was a generational thing: people of my parents' generation (born about 1940) or older wanted their vegetables cooked to a level where they were nice and soft, barely resembling the original ingredient. This has changed over the years as people now accept that al dente is good and it should only be mash if it was meant to be mash; it should never be mush.

For dessert, strawberry crepes would be served in summer. A jar of strawberry jam would be emptied into a saucepan and mixed with some Cointreau or triple sec and allowed to cool. Strawberries were then cut in half and mixed with a little of the jam mix, placed inside the crepe and zapped in the microwave for about 1 minute. It was served dusted with icing sugar and a scoop of Peters vanilla ice-cream. In winter, when strawberries were expensive or unavailable, we would swap to lemon crepes or crepe suzette.

Other desserts which customers expected were chocolate mousse, piped into a saucer champagne glass, top with whipped cream and garnished with a glacé cherry and grated chocolate. If too many champagne glasses were broken we would swap to the stainless steel coupes. Black forest cake was also very common; not the fancy triple-decker thing that would be served nowadays but a very plain black forest cake that we purchased from the local cake shop.

The Didgeridoo, where I started my career, was embarrassing to say the least. As well as crepes and chocolate mousse we served cherries jubilee. A tin of John West black cherries was emptied into a saucepan. Cointreau was added as well as cornflour to thicken, then allowed to cool. To serve, it was heated in the microwave and spooned into a stainless steel coupe with vanilla ice-cream. Finally, there was always fruit salad, also in the stainless steel coupe with whipped cream and a glacé cherry.

By now you are probably thinking I worked in some really bad restaurants. You would be partly right, but mainly wrong: yes, the Didgeridoo by the time I got there in 1982 as an apprentice was a sad restaurant serving sad food to unsuspecting victims, but after that, most of the places I worked in were serving standard fare of the day which you would find in most suburban restaurants. The food itself was, in fact, quite tasty and made by chefs who could actually cook using the traditional principles of cookery.

Many of the dishes served in those days later became unsaleable in a restaurant. Due to their mass production and availability for sale through the supermarkets, things like pâté and, as mentioned before, smoked salmon became so common that a restaurant could no longer just put a few slices on a plate and call it an entrée, nor could they be used for catering purposes either.

People became more sophisticated and, as time went on, chefs needed to be more creative and offer more than just the standard traditional European fare. In the early eighties, the brave new world of fusion (east meeting west) had not occurred to most chefs in Melbourne. For a start, there was very little in the way of Asian ingredients and chefs had very little knowledge of how to use them or the methods of Asian cookery. But by the 1990s, Australia had changed – it had been fifteen to twenty years since the White Australia Policy that kept Australia a largely white European society had ended. Combined with the influx of Vietnamese refugees to Australia in the late seventies, for the first time, we had a sizeable Asian population. And new migrants always bring new food, new tastes and new expectations.

The Grand Hyatt opened in Melbourne in 1987 and a whole swag of young chefs lined up for interviews hoping to work at the new show in town. I was one of them and for the first time I saw a brighter, lighter, fresh approach to food: there were reductions, jus and new ingredients. It was not just the regular, tired, heavy European cuisine that we were all familiar with; it was exciting.

Over time, all those young chefs who had worked at the Hyatt for a couple of years spread out over Melbourne with a new generational attitude to cooking. They were proud and creative; they were chefs with clean white jackets who had survived and thrived in a high pressure, high production, five star environment. Sure, the executive chef was a German, of course, but the chefs de cuisine and sous chefs were Chinese, Indonesian, Irish, English, French and Australian.

It changed my attitude to cooking and opened my eyes to the kind of food that was possible. I remember going to yum cha at a Chinese restaurant one day with other chefs from the Hyatt kitchen and discovering tasty little parcels of heavenly loveliness – wow! How long had this been going on? Little did I know, chefs all over the world had started to think about making use of all these other ingredients and flavours in their own cooking and 'fusion' as a style of cooking took hold, especially in cultural melting pots like Singapore and Hong Kong.

In 1989 Gail and Kevin Donovan left the Hyatt. They took Hong Kong George and Stanley with them to work in the kitchen and opened Chinois Restaurant in South Yarra. I remember going there for dinner and being hooked right from the very start. Chinois encouraged the Asian concept of sharing meals. It was new and revolutionary at the time, as was a Chinese style service and European style food with Asian ingredients. It was a big hit and challenged my thinking as to what was really possible creatively with food – it was so far away from the heavy, classical style of food from my early career. And all of a sudden, I was living the celebrity high life; mixing it with five-star chefs and five-star customers. I hadn't realised life could be this good.

Before long there were Thai, Vietnamese and Japanese restaurants as well as pho cafes and a whole a new generation of Chinese restaurants serving roast duck, char siew pork, steamed pork buns and hot and sour soup. Beef in black bean sauce, special fried rice and lemon chicken were still available on the Aussie/Chinese menu, but for those in the know there was a whole secret menu that the Chinese had always been eating while we had our spring rolls and dim sims.

To give you an idea of the scale of this change, a close friend, Ped, arrived in Australia in 1981 to study architecture at RMIT. He completed his studies and worked as an architect, but like many others he was drawn to the hospitality industry like a seagull is drawn to chips at the MCG. In 1986, Ped opened his first Thai restaurant in Smith Street, Collingwood. At the time, it was the fifth Thai restaurant in

Melbourne – now there are about five hundred in Melbourne alone. We have recently seen a similar explosion of growth in the number of Indian restaurants in the first ten years of this century.

Overall, the eighties ended with a period of culinary enlightenment. A breaking-free from the shackles of the food, chefs, restaurateurs and traditions of the sixties, seventies and early eighties. Gone were the Bavarian oompah bands, the singalongs to 'Roll out the barrel', the chicken à la king, the smorgasbords and the pâté maison – a new breed of home-grown chefs were taking over from the early German and Swiss immigrants. The old style of cooking that we were taught at trade school no longer applied and a whole swag of new ingredients appeared. Chefs started creating a lighter, fresher, more Asian and Italian-influenced style of food – not just in Melbourne and Sydney, but all over the world.

Chapter 4

Spreading my wings

Aside from the Didgeridoo, I completed my apprenticeship at the one suburban restaurant with the same chef and never more than three people in the kitchen. It was time to spread my wings.

A mate from trade school, Martin, was sous chef at an over twenty-fives city nightclub, Lazars. It was a club for mature clients and even had a chef's hat in *The Age Good Food Guide*. In the eighties, people with money liked to splash the cash and Lazars provided a venue where you could have a nice dinner in the restaurant, sit in a quiet corner with a bottle of champagne and dance to the music of the day without drunken eighteen year olds looking to pick up. (It was more like drunken thirty year olds.)

Martin had done really well with stints at the Menzies Hotel, Alexander's and now barely out of his apprenticeship, he was sous chef to a very good chef at Lazars. There were about six of us in the kitchen and the food was still fairly classical but was a big step up from what I had been doing at the Tavern. I went from doing one hundred and twenty covers with three in the kitchen to doing eighty covers with six in the kitchen.

The increase in manpower reflected the complexity of the food. Entrées were baby onion tarts with gorgonzola cheese, hand-sliced smoked salmon from Scotland, hors d'oeuvre platters, and snails were served in little chat potatoes that had been hollowed out then deep fried to crispy little tartlets to hold the snail and the snail butter. We used only King Island unsalted butter and the best of ingredients.

Mains were crayfish thermidor or salad, porterhouse or fillet steak with pepper sauce, madeira jus or beurre maître d'hôtel. Porterhouse steak would be purchased on the bone and hung in the coolroom for three weeks to let it mature and tenderise before being trimmed and portioned (instead of arriving in vacuum pack bags). John Dory fish with capers, giant grilled pork cutlets and stewed apple.

Each main had its own vegetable accompaniment – pommes Anna, pommes gaufrette, potato baskets, mini turned-vegetables, carrot timbales, spinach timbales, Jerusalem artichokes and baby root vegetables such as carrots and turnips – instead of the standard cauliflower and carrots everyone got at the Tavern. We also made a real jus instead of the demi-glace sauce I had been using.

Gone was the chocolate mousse in champagne glasses of my apprenticeship. In its place were Grand Marnier soufflés prepared and cooked to order. Gone was the Peters vanilla ice-cream and instead was the homemade ice-cream from our own ice-cream machine.

Working in a nightclub, I didn't start until 3 pm and would typically be finished by 11 pm (another chef would start later and do the supper). The hours were good, the food was good and we were a great team together. But after about six months, the chef announced he was leaving. Martin was negotiating for the top job, and the owners wanted him, but costs had to come down. I think the catalyst for the whole breakdown was that the restaurant part of the business was losing money and was being subsidised by the nightclub. That's fine when all is well – the restaurant was there for prestige not money – but business is business and nobody likes to see a loss-making department.

When the chef left, as often happens, the whole thing fell in a heap. I was assured of a job but had greater aspirations. We all deserted like rats leaving a sinking ship. Within about three weeks there was only one kitchen brigade member left. New guys were hired and the whole show started again with a new team; that's normal in restaurants in this situation.

From there I was offered a sous chef position at a city restaurant. It was lunch and dinner but the restaurant looked good, the owner was a chef and he had just hired a good new German chef. The complex menu was similar to what I had been doing at Lazars and moreover what I saw myself doing.

It was my chance to really get into cooking good food at a CBD restaurant. I started with great enthusiasm but things didn't seem right. Where was the new German chef? Where was the food that was on the menu? Why were we using frozen crayfish? How could this style of food be made without staff and with second-rate ingredients?

The owner was an English chef who always wore impeccable suits. After the third day, I asked him about the non-existent German only to be informed that he was no longer coming and that he and I would run the kitchen. Knowing full well that the suit was never going to slog it out in the kitchen, I realised I had been conned. At this stage in my career I needed to be with good experienced chefs that I could learn from. I resigned on the spot.

On Monday I went to the agency and got some work to tide me over. It was great knowing that I had the security of agency work when I needed it. If all else failed, I could at least pay the mortgage and put food on the table at home.

Knowing how well my mate Martin had done working at the five-star Menzies Hotel, I decided to apply at the best in town, the Hyatt. Joining the Hyatt was one of the best things I ever did. I was in Plane Tree, the main restaurant in the lobby of the hotel. The kitchen also supplied room service so it was a high-pressure, high-production environment. It was a top class team with top class chefs. There were lots of young cooks like me and we would all drink together after work at Little Reata's or Meitta's in Alfred Place. My chef de cuisine was

Chinese and my sous chef was Indonesian: great guys, the best you could ever hope to work for.

I loved the camaraderie and being part of a five-star team was one of the great experiences of my professional career. We worked hard and under tremendous pressure but it always felt good; things were always happening. I would recommend that all young chefs have a one- or two-year stint at a five-star hotel while they are young. It can set up your career with contacts and credibility.

At the time there was a nightclub at the Hyatt called Monsoons, probably used by businessmen staying at the hotel rather than a place the locals went to. They served Japanese food but didn't really do much business except for a few platters of food to eat with drinks, but because it was a five-star hotel, they needed a real Japanese chef. So this poor guy was brought from Japan and locked in the small kitchen with nobody to talk to, many miles from home in a strange city. But this guy was smart. He knew the currency of chefs and hotel workers: alcohol. He just needed somebody to talk to so he had a supply of sake and snacks for anybody willing to hide out in his kitchen for a while. It was a must to visit him when I did the graveyard shift. Later on at about 4.30 am I would swap my affection to the baker who was by then taking fresh croissants from the oven and offering a shot of Irish whiskey to go with them.

More alcohol could be obtained from the girls in Bar Deco: they would always need lemons and whipped cream for the coffee and drinks. A bit of flirting and a nice smile and I was soon getting dry martinis in a coffee cup.

Yes, life was good, but it can all be taken away at any time: one Sunday night during service we got the news that barely one kilometre up the road a madman had shot up Hoddle Street with an assault rifle, many were killed and we were told not to leave the hotel. The kitchen was silent with shock and disbelief. Melbourne no longer felt safe.

As a chef you always feel that time is ticking away. I had been at the Hyatt for two years and the time had come to fly the coop. There was so much to learn and so little time, but where to next? It's a race from twenty to thirty and if you're not there at thirty, you probably never will be.

Sensing that it was time to move back to restaurants, I got a job at a seafood restaurant in South Yarra with a German chef who also owned the restaurant. It was a good restaurant and good hours so all should have been okay. But I was wrong. Right from the first day I felt like an outsider and in a kitchen of three or four people there is nowhere to hide. After a couple more days I had serious doubts that I would fit in with them, but the food was really good. I really wanted to make it work and learn what he was doing. It was not just the ordinary classical stuff – he was starting to use Japanese ingredients like wasabi and mirin as well as techniques I was eager to learn.

The problem was compounded by the fact that he and his wife were constantly talking in German and often I would sense it was about me.

He was probably a nice guy but in this work situation, his people management skills were low, as they were with most chefs of that era. Over the next few weeks he became more and more critical and less and less friendly. I had been there about three weeks when one Friday night after service he and his wife started a big conversation in German in the kitchen; he was loud and animated. I shut up and cleaned the kitchen but his wife soon returned with an envelope for me. I was sacked.

I felt a wave of relief come over me. I knew it wasn't working but still had a sense of failure and questioned myself. Were they right? Can I be a great chef? Where to next? Combined with the reality of paying the mortgage, car expenses and the electricity bill it was a difficult time, but I vowed never to work for a chef owner ever again and I never did.

It was back to the agency for more casual work then after few phone calls to mates from the Hyatt, I discovered Lenard, a sous chef from the Plane Tree was taking a job as head chef in Mornington. He asked me to join him as his sous chef at a medium-sized venue with a restaurant, function room and about fifty hotel rooms. The function room did mostly weddings, conferences and cabaret nights with local singers and old time rock and roll bands: people my parents' age like Ernie Sigley and Denise Drysdale.

Under normal circumstances the food at this type of venue is average at best, and the rule then was to never eat in a restaurant of a motel. But Lenard was a good chef and we really did do some nice food. He surprised people in the area; Mornington then was not known for its good restaurants. We were doing iced soufflés, spun sugar, scallop savarins, duck galantines in char siew, layered chocolate mousse cakes as well as the standard range of well-known stuff. Lenard was a first generation Australian of Asian background. His father was also a chef at the old Southern Cross Hotel in the sixties, he had a passion for cooking and could create dishes that mixed the classical with some modern thinking.

The owner was an accountant named Frankie. He had run restaurants before and knew how to make money in the restaurant business. An extrovert character, he was always positive and optimistic. A born salesman and socialiser, every Saturday at 12.30 pm he would set up a barbeque at the back of the hotel and the staff would come and have a sausage before work. He would buy the best handmade sausages from a German butcher and have an esky full of beer. Staff and customers staying in the rooms would come down and chat over a sausage and a beer. Frankie had a hard reputation but he was always good to me and was always good to work for.

The bar was run by two guys: Mikey and Nigel. Mikey was a singer in the house band and Nigel was an artist who painted pictures of ships and good ones at that. Both Mikey and Nigel were in the bar for two reasons: free alcohol and sex. Mikey would target the older female customers and Nigel would take the young ones. In hospitality it's generally the barmen who are always at the front of the queue for getting laid, while the chefs get the leftovers. Both could be charming and we were not surprised whenever Mikey would come into the kitchen with a pair of knickers that were given to him by some forty-year-old divorcee at the bar.

It was nice to work there but the workload was heavy – keeping up the mis en place for the two outlets was tough and required long hours. My friend Lenard was obsessed with business and making money, and this made him restless, he only lasted about six months. As for me, the money was good and the location was convenient, but great chefs don't work at motels in Mornington, they work for the Roux brothers in London or at Stephanie's in Hawthorn. I was twenty-five and time was ticking on my career: decisions needed to be made.

I figured that the only real way to get to the top was to go to London or Paris, but it was a high-risk strategy that I never seriously considered. To sell up and drag Joanne across the world for long hours and bad pay was not something that I really wanted to do to me or to her. So at twenty-five I decided I was okay not being a three-hat chef. I had a great relationship with Joanne and maybe a few kids soon and didn't want to work seventy hours a week just to boost my ego. I figured it was better to spend time with her than my sous chef: great chefs have a habit of becoming somewhat one-dimensional as their personal life falls apart around them. They continue to produce great food, but I didn't want to pay that price.

Chapter 5

The money or the plate?

When I left Mornington Lenard and I started a catering business together. We had contracts at a pub and two golf clubs and this enabled us to go into business without the big capital expense of buying a restaurant. But not long after we spilt the company and took a golf club each while ditching the pub.

I worked for six years as a contract caterer at the private golf club under the name Tutti Frutti Catering. When I first started, the Australian economy was going very well and people were spending. People play golf seven days a week so the catering business was busy every day.

Mondays were quiet: I just made sandwiches for sale at the bar. Tuesdays were men's golf day. We would sell pies, pasties and sausage rolls on the course and chips, dim sims, potato cakes and spring rolls were available in the clubhouse after the game. Wednesdays were ladies golf day. They had sandwiches, cakes, cups of tea and various light lunches: it was a high maintenance but low profit day, a necessary evil. Thursdays could be a sandwich day or a corporate day when businesses hired the course for the day and we would supply a two- or three-course meal for lunch or dinner. It was a chance to make some money. Fridays were members' dinner night and we would serve a small menu in the dining room which would change every week. Saturdays were men's day again and we would do the pie and chips thing, then maybe a function like a wedding or party at night. Sunday was a mixed event with light lunches and maybe a dinner in the evening.

It doesn't sound very glamorous but when I started at the club, business was good. I was probably making triple what I could as a chef in a suburban restaurant, and I had a better lifestyle to match. On a quiet day I would go out and play nine holes with the pro or spend the day at the beach. Joanne would help by waitressing on Friday nights, weekends and running front-of-house for the functions.

It's a legitimate question to ask why a real chef would lower himself to chips and steak sandwiches for golfers. For money, of course! I was a lot better off than the $380 I could get in a restaurant. The key to the whole deal was functions: if we could get functions then I would make good money, but if there were no functions, the money was a basic wage only.

Function meals would be alternate serves of two main courses so you could cater to the exact number of customers you were getting paid for.

Most of it was minestrone soup, pumpkin soup, French onion soup or pea and ham soup. Entrées were beef satay, seafood cocktails, smoked salmon. Mains were whole roast porterhouse with mushroom sauce or a chicken breast stuffed with a choice of fillings. Sometimes customers would splash out for fillet of beef wellington or fish of some sort but mostly it was beef or chicken. Desserts were key-lime tart, apple strudel, chocolate mousse, lemon cheesecake, profiteroles with an orange–chocolate sauce or bread and butter pudding, most of it made by me.

All went really well for a couple of years. The local council would hold meetings, cocktail parties and golf days all the time, members would splash out on fortieth birthday parties, presentation and trophy nights and lots of businesses would hold corporate golf days. At Christmas, the midweek men's golfers would have a seafood Christmas dinner. I would fly in about one hundred and twenty fresh crayfish from King Island and along with copious amounts of prawns, oysters and Moreton bay bugs, we would serve an incredible feast.

Members went to the club for dinner all the time and loved my cooking. It was the first time they actually had a professional chef at the club cooking for them and we provided tasty value for money meals that everybody enjoyed. All this and I was making more money than I ever had in my life (and I was only twenty-six).

I developed a love of business rather than straight-out cooking: keeping track of the finances, squeezing every dollar from a function. Making money was now much more fun than cooking and more rewarding. But it all changed on 29 November 1990 when the national treasurer, Paul Keating, announced the recession Australia had to have. I lost fifty per cent of my business overnight. The same thing happened across the whole restaurant business. I lost most of my functions and people swapped a steak sandwich for a bowl of chips. To make matters worse, poker machines had just been introduced into Victoria and people would rather have spent $10 gambling than buying something to eat, and our club didn't have poker machines. I was back to $400 a week, but at least I still had a job.

I decided to ride it out; wait a couple of years for things to sort themselves out then get back to making money again. I resolved to relax, play golf and live a simple lifestyle for a few years. This was harder than it sounds: home mortgage rates were very high, reaching up to eighteen per cent around that time and sending families broke. Many lost their homes. Even big businesses went broke. I just had to sell enough chips, pies and sausage rolls to hang on for two years, I thought. Giving up the golf club gig was not an option because jobs were hard to get, even for chefs.

As the next few years went by I tried all sorts of things to increase turnover. I tried a party platter delivery service that sounded good in theory, but didn't work. There was only one part of the catering business that was booming and that was cheap spit roasts. But most spit roast caterers were not chefs at all. They were butchers, bakers and candlestick makers. The going rate for spit roasts was $5.90 per person and it was a lot of work to prepare, cook, transport, serve and clean up for a hundred people. The only way to make money was to do four functions a night, buy cheap pre-made salads and staff the function with unskilled seventeen-year-olds. This was catering in its lowest form. I didn't mind making chips for golfers but to compete at this low standard was even more than I could bear. I would not do spit roasts.

As happens when money is tight, even the golf club was looking for extra dollars. So they turned their attention to me. They thought I was still making money like I was in the pre-recession era and thought that if the club took over the catering, then they could make that money. Their plan was to squeeze me out: my rent was increased, new demands were made and prices were reduced.

I had to act fast. In financial terms I was going downhill at a rapid rate and couldn't hold out much longer. I had tried everything I could to increase turnover but still it went down. Expenses were going up faster than I could cope with; something had to give. The dream of a successful catering business was now gone. I was losing money and finally, after six years at the club, I was forced to leave.

It was a hard time for my family and I. Our two daughters were four and one and Joanne no longer had a job now the golf club was gone. The mortgage had to be paid, I know I keep saying that but with every pay packet I collected, I would think of the mortgage first. If I fell behind in payments the bank would foreclose and evict my family. I could not afford for this to happen under any circumstances. It was the number one bill that got paid every month; everything else came second.

But out of adversity comes prosperity. As it turned out, they did me a favour. I would have stayed a lot longer and got more and more tied to the job and the club if they had not forced the issue. When you have your back to the wall you do your best thinking.

I started to look for a job in a restaurant again, but found that even with fifteen years' experience and five-star hotel experience the offers were very poor. The Hyatt offered me a job but I couldn't afford to take it. I had a friend who worked in a supermarket getting more money than I was being offered – not a manager, just an ordinary worker. In a good restaurant I could be a chef de partie or a head chef in a pub or suburban restaurant. But the pubs and suburban restaurants didn't really want to hire a previously self-employed caterer as a head chef, even one with a good resume.

In the end I found a chef de partie job at a beach-side restaurant owned by previous Hyatt people. If you can handle working in the Plane Tree then you can handle anything. I really did enjoy cooking good food again and being part of a kitchen brigade was great after working by myself for so long. The food was good but the pay was poor and the hours were long. To save money I would eat all my meals at work and park for free about one kilometre away from the restaurant. Breaks were a coffee from work and a walk on the beach. I could go a whole week without spending any money except for petrol.

What they don't tell you when you are watching *MasterChef* or when you go to culinary school is that when you do get qualified and start to work as a cook you will be faced with a big decision. The money or the food! Everything is a trade off in this industry.

If you decide that the food is the most important thing then you will seek to work at the better restaurants for the rock star chefs. You will learn great cooking techniques, produce some great food and have the prestige of saying you've worked there. You may even decide to pack up and work in Europe for a few years to gain experience. All of this will help build your skills, build your resume and maybe turn you into a great chef. But don't expect to get paid for the privilege.

If a restaurant or chef is the hottest in town, many cooks will want to work for them for the learning experience and to have it on their resume; not the money. And with fierce competition for jobs, the restaurant doesn't need to pay well. Cooks will in general work flat out in a fast-paced, high-intensity, testosterone-fuelled kitchen until they are burnt out and discarded and replaced by another doe-eyed youth with dreams of being the next rock star. The cooks that take these jobs know the rules of the game, they know how things work – and are perfectly willing players in the game. To be fair, some do go on to be the next generation of rock star chefs but ninety-nine per cent will end up with a great resume, great skills and should be very proud of their achievements, but that's about all.

After the Hyatt, Shannon Bennett packed up and went to Europe. He worked long hours in the best kitchens for poor money and became a great chef. When I left the Hyatt I could have gone overseas as well but I was married and was paying off a house. I didn't to want change my whole life plan. Maybe if I had, I might also have been a rock star. No, not really! For every one who makes it, there are a thousand great chefs who never get recognised, never get the fame and never get the money. That is if they even become great chefs at all. Most wouldn't even make it to that stage. It's just too hard, too demanding and you must give up everything else in life to even give it a shot. That wasn't for me.

The other route you can take is to work for whoever pays you the most, a culinary mercenary so to speak. Once you start down this road you have to understand that you can't all of a sudden swap to the good food rock-star side of the business. You are locked in. There are some chefs working in so-called Italian restaurants producing very average food on really great salaries. Why? It's not because they are great cooks, because they are not; it's because they do three hundred and fifty covers on a Friday night and another three hundred and fifty on a Saturday night. Low food cost and high turnover leads to high profits. If a chef is a gun at preparation and can handle the fast hectic service to pump out three hundred and fifty covers in two and a half to three hours then he is worth good money to the restaurant owner. Pay him well, keep him happy and have fewer problems.

The same thing went for me. I had the opportunity to cook basic, simple food and get paid a lot more than if I had worked at the three-hat restaurants. So I took the money and paid the mortgage. It was a very personal decision – which path would you choose?

Chapter 6

Hitting the wall

It's 1996 and about 3.30 pm on a Sunday afternoon. It's a hot summer's day and I am sitting at St Kilda beach pumping caffeine into my body via a double strength cafe latte. I'm worried, very worried. I've just been slammed on the grill and wok for a two-hundred cover Sunday lunch at the busy beachside restaurant where I work as a chef de partie. Sunday is the busiest day of the week and we get hammered hard for lunch and dinner.

Keeping up with the cleaning and portioning of fish, the macadamia crust for the blue eye, the chilli sauce for the crab, the jus for the steaks, the lime butter in the oysters, the sashimi garnishes, beurre blanc, black bean concentrate, Noilly Prat velouté and turned vegetables is impossible. I have already run out of most items or garnishes. Sure, I have raw ingredients, but to turn those raw ingredients into mis en place takes time and manpower and that's exactly what I don't have. Other chefs in the kitchen are in exactly the same situation.

The exec chef is a great guy and a really good chef but I don't expect any help from him to prepare my mis en place. The best I can hope for is that the sous chef stops socialising with a table of young women in the courtyard and gets his arse in the kitchen to help me. Maybe he will and maybe he won't. I catch his eye with a look of despair on my face and he reluctantly ambles over. I have a quiet word to him about the state of my battlefield. He realises that he can't afford my section to go down mid service so he turns off his fantasy brain and turns on his kitchen brain and helps me with the mis en place, saving me from disaster and embarrassment.

It's a beautiful day at the beach; a hive of leisure, pleasure and activity. This is really bad news for me because at 5.30 pm the ratchet noise of the printer above my station will start issuing dockets and will not stop until about 10 pm. Each table expects great food in a timely manner, and even with the sous chef helping with the mis en place, any one of a thousand things could go wrong. If I lose five or ten minutes of cooking time or overcook a few orders on the grill, the whole service will collapse like a house of cards. I could have four other cooks, two chefs, three waiters and one of the owners all looking at me to put up food that is not yet cooked. Sweat will be running down my cheek and I will be able to feel and count every loud, fast, heartbeat in my body like the ticking of a clock. Tick tock, tick tock. Seconds become minutes and I just want it to end. Like an army general, the chef may be required to send more troups to help out the area under attack, and like a war it may help and it may not, but if your section is the weak link then you are the weak link and your career is on the line if it happens too often.

I sit at the beach on my sole twenty-minute break for the day contemplating all this. I'll do fourteen hours today; twelve yesterday and thirteen on Friday. I'm thirty-two years old and have been doing this for fourteen years. I'm on a salary so there's no overtime for me. The salary is okay, but when you look at the hours I'm doing the only conclusion you can draw is that I am little more than a paid slave.

This is what happens when you hit the wall. I knew it would happen one day. All chefs know it will happen one day, but today is my day. What is happening to my life? *I* should be sitting there on the beach playing with my kids. *I* should be rollerblading along the foreshore. *I* should be a customer in the restaurant sometimes. Will life always be like this? Will it always be *other* people drinking, eating, swimming, laughing and living life? Will I always be working twelve or fourteen hours a day?

I could see my life spiralling into the bitter and socially inept life of an old bastard chef: drinking too much, working long hours and spending most of the time complaining about everything from rap music to how young cooks think they know it all. I could see the train speeding along and knew that I had to get off before I reached that final, lonely, bitter destination.

I made a decision right then that things had to change. I sat down a few days later and had a good look at my skills and myself. What could I do? What did I have to offer? Not much, really! I could cook and – what else? I knew I was never going to be the hot-shot chef about town on the hot-shot salary consulting to three restaurants and doing a spot on daytime television once a month. In chef terms, I wasn't sexy, I had no overseas experience, no three-hat experience, I was Australian born and bred. I could cook but I was not a star and never would be and at thirty-two, with a family, I had quite correctly passed up the opportunity of Paris or London but that had left me with little room to move and a diminishing number of places to work.

I decided I needed to move on from cooking in the kitchen. I had tried business and that worked for a time, but didn't end well. But where to now, and how? I was too old to start again in a whole new industry. I really did love cooking though and the hospitality industry so decided I needed more training in other aspects of the industry. Working twelve hours a day in this situation I could never get the training or move forward in any real way. So I came to the conclusion that I had to leave the beachside restaurant and change to a job with a larger corporate opportunity.

Crown Casino was the biggest game in town. They had been open for about a year at the temporary site at the World Trade Centre and were building up to the opening of their $2 billion new casino on the banks of the Yarra River at Southbank. Their appetite for chefs was insatiable and they were soaking up all the available chefs in town as well as importing top-line staff from all over the world.

I knew that if I could join Crown at the sous chef level I would have access to training and be part of the opening team; something that is looked upon in the industry as very prestigious and valuable. At opening you are under enormous pressure but you get to see other business aspects of the industry that you normally wouldn't see, so I knew it would help me.

I applied to Crown as a sous chef and had an appointment directly with the executive chef. He looked at my resume and asked some questions about my current role at the beachside restaurant. 'What does quality mean to you?' he asked. I answered that quality was not necessarily haute cuisine and that a sandwich could be quality if it was made well. He seemed to like the answer and saw that I had worked two years at the Grand Hyatt.

'If you can work for two years for Bruno at the Grand Hyatt, you can work for me,' he said. It appeared that executive chef was a Hyatt man. (Chefs often identify themselves by the places where they have worked.) I had the job. He wanted me to start as a senior chef (chef de partie) and go into a management training program straight away. This was exactly what I was after. He promised to reconsider the position after I had completed management training and after about eight weeks, he promoted me to sous chef.

I was allocated to the Santé Brasserie, a busy lobby-type restaurant open 24 hours a day. About half the chefs were of Asian background while the others were a mixed bag of Australians and Europeans. There were two other sous chefs with me and my chef de cuisine was a big black man from Sri Lanka known as 'the bull'.

Working at Crown was not like working at any other restaurant or even any other hotel: it was the most intense job I had ever had. It was a big-time production serving up to 1500 covers a day with a half-Asian, half-western menu. There was the usual hawker-style food, roast duck and rice, char siew and rice, congee, Sichuan beef, char kway teow and soy chicken. The western-style food was a collection of steaks, grilled chicken with salsa, pre-made fish and chips, grilled salmon, prawn cocktails, a couple of pastas and oysters natural. There was also the buffet and carvery lunches for the busloads of people transported in from all over the state day after day to play the poker machines: roast beef, baked potatoes, coleslaw, potato salad, bean salad, mustard and cakes for dessert; all the usual suspects.

At the time Crown was about the size of a large five-star hotel and operated at full speed 24 hours a day. However, because of the gambling and the need to pamper the high rollers everything was more intense. If a player was gambling tens of thousand dollars every blackjack hand and wanted dolphin on toast then it was our job to get him that dolphin on toast and it must be exactly right. Any mistakes and the execs were all over you like a rash, next day you're frying chips in the sports bar.

One day we had a high roller who wanted orange segments, so we carefully segmented some oranges and arranged them on a plate as per the instructions. Fifteen minutes later the host was back asking for bigger segments. We searched the whole casino and found some bigger oranges, segmented them and arranged them again. Half an hour later, they were back again; not sweet enough. The exec sous then spent an hour on the phone with suppliers and flew in two boxes of large, sweet oranges from Darwin. In the meantime, we improvised by soaking segments in sugar syrup. Seven hours later, the high roller was still gambling and still wanting large, sweet, orange segments. The Darwin boxes arrived and we prepared the new segments that were finally approved. It may seem extravagant, but if the gambler has lost $350 000 in the meantime, who really cares how much the orange segments cost!

At a venue like Crown, from a chef's point of view, the only things you need to worry about are food production, service, food/cost percentage and staff issues. Food production is difficult because you are turning over so much food but you have limited storage and refrigeration space. Your mis en place is wiped out every day. In Santé, we had a graveyard shift starting at 11 pm to do the mis en place: without this, we couldn't have operated. The graveyard shift was led by a cook named Robert, and he was a gun for preparation. He was fast and accurate: you could give him a prep list at 11 pm and when the guys got in the next morning it would all be done. I would never know how it was done and I would never ask.

But Robert was high maintenance. Every night he would lecture me about all the things that were wrong with the place and which chefs were dickheads. Then he would ask me when was he getting a day shift roster. It would take all my newly attained people skills from my management course to steer Robert through another night pointed in the right direction, my direction. I knew he needed massaging and a kind word, not abuse. Robert may have been a pain in the arse but he was our pain in the arse and without him the night work was often not done.

Some production was done for us in the garde manger kitchen (which catered to the whole casino), but that necessitated that we place our orders on time and be nice to them. Service takes care of itself if all the production is done and the mis en place is ready. If you have the right guys on the right equipment then generally, it will all be okay. In a busy restaurant such as this there are two guys to work the pass. One on the kitchen side of the service bench to plate the food, give final inspection and instruction to the cooks and to communicate with the guy on the restaurant side of the pass whose job it is to coordinate between the kitchen and the front of house. He will call away tables, watch the timing of every docket, handle changes and complaints, call waiters, tell waiters which guest has which meal and give all food a final inspection.

Front-of-house staff don't talk to the kitchen, they talk to the chef on the pass. A high-level chef usually works the pass and what he says goes. If he rejects a meal on a table of eight he can send the whole table back to the kitchen to be replaced. High-pressure stuff when you are trying to pump out four hundred meals. The bull, me or another sous chef would usually work the pass on the restaurant side but if it was really busy, an exec sous would take over and we would help the cooking section which was getting slammed.

The food/cost percentage is the number that chefs live and die by. You can do a good job cooking nice food, keeping up with the mis en place, getting lovely guest comments and be a well-liked chef among your peers, but if your food/cost percentage is too high, you will have a very short career.

The food/cost percentage is calculated by adding up all the money you spend on food and dividing it into the sales you have made and then expressing it as a percentage. In Santé, we had a food/cost target of about forty per cent. Normally, a chef would be sacked long before it got to forty per cent, but we were a casino and prices were deliberately cheap as we were subsidised by the gaming department.

The food/cost report came out every day. At the 9.30 am chef's meeting I would need to report our food cost. If it was above target I would need to explain why, and what we were doing to bring the cost back to target. It was said that a one per cent food cost for the whole casino was worth about $1 million at the time, so it was important.

So how do you control the food cost? Food cost may be high because you have a lot of stock on hand. This would be normal on a Friday morning, but if it were high on a Monday morning then there would be a problem because you will have had the weekend sales and stock should be low. Or, you can keep a close eye on the cost of ingredients. For example, if tomatoes are expensive, take the tomato salad off the buffet and replace it with a cucumber salad that will be much cheaper. Next, you must ensure that you have very little waste by not over producing, or by controlling portions. You can also place low food cost but popular dishes on the specials list; this will bring down the costs and make the figures look better. Or, you can steal food from other kitchens. What! Do chefs really steal from each other? Oh yeah, big time. You must patrol your kitchen and food storage areas like a military officer to eliminate or reduce theft from your kitchen.

In most hotels – and Crown Casino was no different – it was the job of the overnight guys to steal what they could to help reduce the food cost. A 3 am trip to the garde manger may yield sides of smoked salmon, a case of rockmelons, boxes of tomatoes or lemons, bags of frozen prawns – the list was endless. But by morning, when the day guys arrive, the evidence has already been destroyed: the lemons are already lemon wedges in your coolroom, the prawns are already defrosted and part of the marinara mix in the pasta section … you get the idea.

Both the bull and I were experienced in this form of pilfering from our days at the Hyatt. Stealing from other kitchens was expected and all part of the game and, of course, other chefs would also try to steal from us.

It wasn't just food we would steal, though. When I did the graveyard shift at the Hyatt, my job was to raid the whole hotel and report gains to the sous chef in the morning. Pans, spoons and trays were in-demand items. There were never enough trays so we would steal what we could and lock up a secret stash for when we needed them. Glad wrap and foil are great finds when you're on the prowl. Anybody stupid enough to leave a roll of glad wrap lying around after hours deserves for it to be stolen. Don't bother writing your outlet on the box, I'll just throw the box away and keep the roll. Write on the roll itself, I'll steal it anyway.

Each night at Santé the pastry cook would come to our kitchen for his dinner of chilli prawns. They were placed in a stainless steel food container as if they were something else, and he would go downstairs to the pastry kitchen, hide in a dark corner and eat his dinner. When the order for our kitchen would come up from his section, there would be a few extra cakes on the trolley, but not on the docket. It would all add up to help reduce the pressure on the food cost. Most chefs have no problems partaking in such practices as the suits often place unrealistic expectations on the food cost that cannot be achieved so the chefs are really just playing the game, the suits get the bonus and everyone is happy.

The main staff issue in a place like this is just trying to keep the staff motivated enough to keep the machine going. To do this, if you have twenty-five cooks in your kitchen, you need to know why each one of them is there. What do they want? What are they trying to achieve? Some cooks are ambitious and want to be promoted; others simply want overtime and money; some want to work in the more prestigious restaurants.

Whatever they want, it is the job of the chef de cuisine and sous chef to manage each person according to their needs. They work hard and if they see no movement in their career plan then you are the one who suffers. They must feel appreciated, valued and know that you understand and support their career plan. You need to take a *genuine* interest and look after those who look after you.

For the opening of the Southbank complex I was allocated to Conservatory, the main restaurant in the lobby of the Crown Towers Hotel. It was quite a prestigious job. The bull was allocated to the position of chef de cuisine. The new casino complex had about thirty-five restaurants and food outlets so there were hundreds of cooks and chefs.

The Conservatory was a complex restaurant, very complex. It had five different menus, an à la carte menu for lunch and dinner, a breakfast menu, a high-tea menu, a lobby-bar snacks menu and a buffet lunch and dinner with a fourteen-day rotating menu. There were about nineteen kitchen staff over a seven-day roster. With that number of cooks and that number of menus and dishes, I knew it couldn't be done in that exact format, not to the standard required anyway. It would be need to simplified. I knew there would be blood on the floor, probably my blood and I was right.

The bull was a keen observer and master of organisation. He was across every management detail and political machination, not just in Santé but across the whole casino. He knew every person in the whole complex from the CEO to the kitchen steward by name. I didn't know it straight away, but being assigned to him was stroke of luck – he's not just a great chef and taught me a great deal about the role of a sous chef, he is a reader of people.

He acquired the name the bull when he started at Crown. He worked like a machine. No hours were too long for him: he could work sixteen hours a day, every day, without complaining once. A big solid man, he played hard, worked hard and was a force to be reckoned with. Almost everybody likes and respects him. And he could charm you into anything. At the Hyatt, he had been known affectionately as 'Cookie', but to me he was always the bull. I consider him a brother and am still very close to him despite the fact that we have not worked together for around ten years.

The bull always refers to cooking in a military manner. Preparing mis en place is 'preparing for battle', dockets off the printer are like 'flying bullets' and looking after his staff is 'taking care of your soldiers'. He approaches the job in fine detail and a keen sense of 'us or them'. He has a long memory with a long list of names; each name has tick or a cross beside it. If it's a tick then he will do anything for you or to protect you. But if it's a cross, he will make you suffer big time and you may never know it was him. Revenge and loyalty are traits the bull prides himself upon.

As his sous chef in Santé and for the Conservatory I was the bull's right hand man. The basic role of a sous chef is to do everything that a chef doesn't have time to do. Problems should not get elevated to the attention of the chef. Order the food, fix the equipment, counsel the staff, steal the food, cover his back, do whatever it takes – you are his wingman; his life depends on you.

But the bull is a practical man, not an office man. He had opened hotels before and knew what to do, but documenting it on a computer was not his strength. So I did the bulk of this work for the opening plan for Conservatory. With the exec sous chefs reporting everything back to the executive chef, the bull couldn't hide the fact that paperwork was not his forte.

Once we had two weeks to produce a master plan of documents for the opening of Conservatory to present to the executive chef for approval. I did most of the work while the bull concentrated on running Santé. One exec sous watched us like a hawk. We delivered the plan on time, but this guy was keen to make a good impression on the exec chef – and he wasn't happy that I made the documents and not the bull. He got in the exec chef's ear and convinced him that the bull was not up to the task and the bull was removed from Conservatory.

This was a defining moment in the bull's life and for me, too – I could see that corporate life was not for me. The bull had worked harder than anybody, had all the experience, all the credentials to prove he could do the job, but in the end it didn't matter; they still discarded him like an off oyster. They put him on the night shift hoping to get rid of him, but he wasn't called the bull for nothing. He would leave on his terms, not theirs. He stayed at Crown for another year and eventually, like me, took a redundancy payout and moved on. He would never again work for a hotel; he had played the hotel game for twenty-five years and was tired.

The pre-planning and building of the new complex was watched over by an army of executive sous chefs. They patrolled the kitchens and restaurants like the East German Stasi and reported our every move back to the demi gods with the real power. If even a simple mistake was made, someone had to take a bullet; someone had to be transferred; someone was now a fry cook or a snack bar attendant on the suffer-till-you-die roster. It's a basic fundamental rule of the hotel business, but it was especially so at Crown.

The opening went well but the venue was so high profile that everyone was on edge and pushing, pushing and pushing for higher and higher standards. If the ice-cream was low on the buffet, the coolroom was untidy, a sticker was found on a mango at the buffet, somebody had to take the blame. There was a climate of instability and suspicion among the staff and the frequent forced transfers to other areas or outright sackings of chefs, restaurant managers and even those higher up on a weekly basis meant that the paranoid delusions were not delusions at all – you're not paranoid if people really are out to get you, you're just observant.

Being sacked from or transferred within a prestigious hotel like Crown is a huge personal blow to a chef. To be transferred to a bulk cooking outlet means that your career there is over and you will be viewed as having failed. The demotion shows on your resume and it indicates that you could not make the grade. It's a stain, a big stain. Chefs define their self worth by the standard of the restaurant where they work. To make matters worse many of us had been working on a project for a year or more, and to have it taken away from us just after opening was demoralising, to say the least.

With good men falling around me, I knew that one day I too would be moved on, so best to get in and get what you want and get out. Anyway, about three weeks after opening, a chef de partie and I were called into the office and told we were out of Conservatory. I could do nothing other than say, 'Yes, chef'. To do anything else would cost my reputation; if they wanted to, they could have trashed my name at every major hotel in Melbourne. I knew the rules and how to play: 'Yes, chef!'

That chef de partie is now one of the best chefs in Melbourne, low profile, but a man of extraordinary culinary skills. Unfortunately, the Conservatory burned through about four chefs de cuisine and five sous chefs (including me) in the space of about three months after opening before the penny dropped that maybe the set up was wrong. In building Conservatory, some crucial things were ignored in the planning process. The kitchen had no freezer; there were no staff toilets in that part of the building and there were no computers to place orders or approve staff timesheets.

All this meant you were out of the kitchen doing administration work for long periods while the Stasi patrolled the premises like German shepherds in a scrap metal yard. In pre-opening planning, the menus were made by the executive sous chefs and given to us completed. Then came about a week of trialling the recipes and playing with the presentation of each dish. The execs, the bull, another sous chef and I would plate each dish, discuss the portion and presentation, make adjustments then take a photo and lock it in as final. With over a hundred dishes it took a long time and with other tasks to be completed, it often required sixteen-hour days.

The opening was delayed for a long time so we found ourselves working in the office doing planning for six months. Making a list for this, a list for that, inputting over six hundred recipes into the computer. Training plans, equipment plans, safety plans, take-over plans, specials plans, the lists went on and on.

We had an entire floor of another building in the World Trade Centre site dedicated to the chefs. A whole floor full of desks and computers – and an armada of chefs to do the planning. It was 1997 and chefs used computers to place orders and approve timesheets and so on using specific hotel-type software, but most had little or no experience at all with Microsoft Word, Microsoft Excel or email.

There were only a couple of guys who actually had some basic computer skills including myself. It was a time of great confusion as well as excitement. We were not really sure what we were doing. We would work all day producing a document such as a list of all the equipment in our kitchen and then we would print the document and give a copy to an exec sous chef (we never used email). After long, careful consideration, the exec sous would say that it was fine, but could we indent this text or make that a double line instead of a single line.

We would then go back to our desk and play with Excel for another three hours to work out how to change the document to give the presentation he wanted. Not really sure why it was so important to have the text indented or a double line, but I was assured it was all very important at the time. They were obviously working on the theory that if you give enough typewriters to enough monkeys, eventually you will get *Hamlet*.

After Conservatory I was put in Winners, a 24-hour restaurant on the casino gaming floor. Winners was again a high-production kitchen serving nice food but nothing special. This was fine with me. I had long since lost my desire to play the survival of the fittest game, I could play with the big boys alright but I no longer wanted to.

The Winners job was easier than Conservatory but far less prestigious. Everyone thought of it as a demotion, but to me, it was great because it allowed me to cruise. My chef de cuisine was a Greek guy named Christakos; he played by his own rules and was good to work for.

Christakos was not like most of the other chefs. He was not from a five-star background and had never worked at a hotel before. Most chefs define themselves as a Hyatt man, a Hilton man, a Dorchester Hotel man or a Taj Hotel chef but not him, he wasn't concerned with such rigmarole. He was proud and confident. A production chef who could produce vast amounts of food at average Italian-type bistros in busy tourist areas. You couldn't help but like him for his honesty and the fact that he always looked after his staff and got the job done. If you worked in a canteen serving six hundred for lunch and another four hundred for dinner, Christakos would be the man you would want standing beside you. A gun at prep and a calm head for any service. When you worked for Christakos, he would always look out for you and treat you well.

He joined Crown just for a look, really, to see what a big corporate hotel-type situation was like. Because he had no intention of making a career at Crown or in the hotel world, he did not play the political game with the execs. They had nothing over him so they could not completely control him. He would tell the Stasi to fuck off and there was nothing they could do. Sack him, move him, reprimand him; it was all water off a duck's back. He was quite prepared to go back to food production at the cafe.

When he opened Winners, he needed to set up a display area for the food (fish on ice, oysters, steaks, chicken etc) to show how fresh it was. As time went on, each executive sous chef would come and tell him to change the display, move the fish over there, move the steaks behind the fish etc. After having this go on for a while Christakos had had enough. He would leave the glass display case empty.

The executive chef walked past and enquired why there was no display. Christakos let him have it with both barrels. It was fuck this and fuck that and there was no setting up of the display until the exec sous chef fucked off out of the restaurant. Everyone was stunned. You didn't talk to the executive chef like that; cooks were expecting for him to be sacked on the spot, but he wasn't. The executive chef just looked at him and said, 'You set up the display however you want.'

The Stasi never touched him again. Here was a man not even afraid of the executive chef. Respect!

Once Christakos had seen enough of the corporate hotel and casino world he left and went back to the production cafe. He is well known in those circles and has the ability to work under his own rules (high wages, starts work when he wants, ends work when he wants and no-one tells him what to do) because he always gets the job done. Lots of restaurants and cafes want Christakos to work for them and all are willing to accept the rules as long as he will accept a job at their restaurant. If he gets bored or you break the rules then he's gone. It's not the type of chef people aspire to be, but it works well for him.

From Winners I went to Georges, the pizza restaurant next door. That was great fun working with a large, wood-fired pizza oven. It was a casual and relaxed atmosphere drinking lattes, chatting to customers and cooking pizza, with the gaming floor as entertainment. We had plenty of staff and the food was simple but nice.

Eventually I think they discovered I was enjoying myself in Georges and shifted me to run the snack bars. At first I thought it would be dead boring, but I wasn't working the fryers, I was running the food part: six or seven snack bars with about fifty cooks in my area. I would place orders, supervise staff, plan specials, look after quality control and mediate the arguments. The job changed me from the kitchen brigade into the Casino Food and Beverage (F&B) department, reporting to the F&B manager.

It was like running a catering business again: looking at takings, profits, food/cost percentages, gross profits etc. It presented a whole new set of exciting challenges.

One Sunday morning, I was walking past the three, big floor-to-ceiling sports screens in the casino sports bar and saw the mangled wreck of a black Mercedes. Running across the bottom of the screen were the words, 'Paris – Diana Crash; Dodi Dead.' Casinos never go quiet, I mean never. But all of a sudden the whole sports bar stopped and looked at the screen. Old, crusty sports gamblers were frozen in their tracks and fixated on the screen. Half an hour later it read: 'Diana Dead!' Gamblers approached me and asked me about the screen. 'Is it a movie?' 'No it's real, Diana's dead.' I rang Joanne and told her to turn on the TV, Diana was dead. We were all stunned.

After about six months hiding out in snack bars they were laying off a lot of staff from the whole complex with redundancy packages – a concept whereby you pay people large amounts of money not to come to work. This appealed to me greatly. I figured it was time to cash the cheque and move on. Maybe I wasn't really a corporate man, after all.

Chapter 7

Culinary entertainment

During my career, even while I was learning the traditional dishes and methods of cookery, cookery itself was changing: after one hundred years of cooking essentially the same style of food, slowly the ingredients were changing, restaurants were changing and customers were changing.

Once upon a time food was just for eating. At some stage in the early nineties, food started to become art, and then in the new century, food started to become entertainment. It was very hard just to keep up. I managed to keep up with the transformation from food to art but did not manage to keep up with the progression from art to entertainment. I was caught in the middle of a generational change and like others before me in such a situation, I found myself cooking classical music while the new generation cooked rock and roll.

Not so long ago, the chef was kept away from the general public. On occasion, he was brought out to say hello to the VIP guest while the maître d' held his breath hoping that the chef would say all the right things and disappear back into the kitchen as soon as possible. Chefs had no media training, no customer service training and were generally not interested in customers beyond them being a number on a docket.

Waiters were often in a difficult position when a guest had a special request. It might be possible or it might not. If it was busy, the chef might look the waiter in the eye and flatly say, 'Tell the customer to go get fucked.' The chef would know that the waiter would not actually tell the guest to get fucked but it was symptomatic of the role and mood of the chef, locked in the back room. We were there to produce food and food production was and is the name of the game. This was my era of kitchens: we worked hard, prepared food, drank too much and told everybody, 'Fuck you, I'm the chef.'

In the nineties, new ingredients started to become available and the dominance of the German and Swiss chefs started to diminish. A new breed of young Australian chefs came on the scene and top quality Asian chefs started to come to Australia.

One of the biggest changes at the time was the introduction of hydroponic lettuces: butter lettuce, coral lettuce and red oak were a revelation. In the eighties, we worked with iceberg, curly endive and cos lettuce – that was it! Then with the introduction of hydroponic mesclun salad leaves in all their different shapes it was like the discovery of penicillin: we had rocket, mizuna, lamb's lettuce, radicchio and various other baby lettuce leaves.

All this made a huge difference to the presentation of food in restaurants. Suddenly we had chefs starting to take more of an interest in food presentation. A half, van-dyke lemon was replaced with half a lemon that was dipped in sugar and grilled or deep-fried chips of sweet potato and beetroot. Parsley became a sign that you were yesterday's man.

The ingredients we were using also started to change. When I was an apprentice we used vegetable oil, walnut oil and almond oil; we hardly ever used olive oil, even for a salad. Butter was the main sauté medium. Because of this, food was heavier and more classical.

When we started to use olive oil, food become lighter and had a fresher Mediterranean taste and style about it rather than the heavy style of the colder climate European countries. Replacing things like a heavy demi-glace with a jus of a concentrated flavour also made for a lighter, more pleasant sauce.

In the eighties and nineties, nobody used balsamic vinegar: we used white wine vinegar, champagne vinegar, red wine vinegar and raspberry vinegar. Balsamic quickly became the dominant vinegar in cooking and on tables with good quality extra virgin olive oil and some gourmet breads. It changed everything.

Food was becoming art and menus changed accordingly. Seafood cocktails and pâté maison became old fashioned and were replaced with more creative entrées. Chocolate mousse served in a champagne glass became a layered chocolate marquise served with almond tuille and macerated cherries.

At the same time, the Kaiser Stuhl rosé and Ben Ean moselle my parents drank was replaced with quality Australian chardonnay from areas like the Yarra Valley. Wine started to become important and for the first time Australians started to drink table wine on a regular basis. Before that, Dad drank beer and Mum drank a strange cocktail of Advocaat and lemonade. In the eighties, a full liquor licence to sell alcohol was expensive and difficult to obtain so most people brought their own. But by the nineties, most restaurants were licensed to sell alcohol.

About that time, plates also started to get bigger: an 8-inch entrée plate became a 10-inch entrée plate; a 10-inch main course plate became a 12-inch main course plate. This increase in size gave chefs room to create a picture, match the colours, add complex garnishes and add a personal touch to the food.

We started to see lots of new words on the menu too: mayonnaise became aioli; verjuice, chermoula, dukkha, salsa and gremolata all arrived on printed menus; jus and pancetta were born; rouille was discovered; and crisscross grill marks on food became important.

In the cutting-edge, molecular-gastronomy world the baby mesclun lettuce leaves have been replaced with micro herbs of radish, parsley, basil, mibuna, komatsuna, cabbage and red basil. Placed on the plate almost piece by piece, I've even seen chefs use tweezers to place them on the plate. Tweezers? Really? We use to throw garnishes on the plate, wipe the rim and yell, 'Take away table five!'

Ingredients are no longer flavoured, they are 'infused' as in 'truffle-infused, sugar-gum honey from Kangaroo Island'. Even simple honey is no longer good enough, it must be infused with an exotic flavour. We also need to be told which trees the bees collected the nectar from and where the trees were at the time. Only then can we really enjoy the roast pumpkin and spinach salad that has been caramelised with this magnificent and very, very special honey.

In the past bacon, smallgoods and salmon were smoked. You could get cheap, frozen, smoked cod to eat on Good Friday and that's about all. Now any manner of ingredients are smoked – beetroot is smoked; fresh meats are smoked; vegetables are grilled and smoked; even eggs and butter are smoked. And they're not just smoked with any ordinary wood; there's apple wood, hickory, mesquite, cherry wood, alder wood, maple, oak or pecan wood.

Beef is no longer beef; we need to know where the beef came from, how old the animal was, what they ate (grass or grain) and how many days the beef has been aged for as in, 'Cape Grim dry-aged, 36-month-old, grass-fed rib-eye on the bone, 350 g, 78 + days: $60'.

Food is exactly cut into cubes, rectangles or geometric shapes and placed millimetre-perfect on the plate, mini vegetables to match, a foam of some sort and splashes or swishes of three different-coloured sauces or oils.

Soup is served in a test tube as an amuse bouche. I repeat, a test tube! Until a couple of years ago I had never even heard of an amuse bouche let alone knew what one was. Now it's standard and everybody discusses it as if they have been making them all their life.

Food was moving at such a pace only those chefs at the cutting edge could keep up with it. I could cook, but these new ingredients and methods were beyond the scope of all but a few cooks of my generation. I would see new words on a menu all the time. Friends would ask me, 'What is black garlic?' I don't know! 'What is togarashi spice?' I don't know! 'What does kelp taste like?' *I don't know!* To even attempt to keep up you had to live and breathe cooking, read every magazine and go to every hot-shot new restaurant. Otherwise you wouldn't know how to make 'mushroom powder' to sprinkle on pasta.

Food, however, is now firmly in the realm of entertainment. The degustation menu is the ultimate form of food porn and culinary entertainment. Your choice is a night at the theatre seeing the new production of *Mary Poppins* or *The Jersey Boys*, or the ten-course degustation menu at the fine dining restaurant of the latest celebrity chef.

You can't just eat a degustation menu, each dish needs to be explained by the waiter, each accompanying wine needs to be carefully articulated and matched with the food by the sommelier. Each dish is explained, viewed, discussed, eaten and then discussed again.

It's like the step-up from normal, married couple sex to special effort holiday sex. First you see and admire the object of your desire, imagining what will happen. Then the undressing is like the waiter's explanation of each part of the dish: as each layer is removed, as each word is spoken, you understand and appreciate the prize even more. Until the final delicate devouring of the complete dish which leaves you feeling satisfied and a little bit special – but hungry for more.

Soon they will be selling menus with articles on the kitchen staff, a profile of the chef, a history of the dishes and the philosophy of the restaurant. It will be just like when you buy a program at the theatre or ballet. Guests will get the chef to sign the program. Junior *MasterChef*-type kids will collect them like swap cards. 'I'll swap you one Neil Perry for a Kylie Kwong.'

Chefs are already performing in theatres. Chefs like Rick Stein at the Melbourne Regent Theatre, Jamie Oliver Live at the Hisense Arena and Guy Grossi invented a show called, 'In the raw: dinner and live show with Guy Grossi and Luke Mangan'. Guy starred in his own cabaret-style production on stage with Luke. Cooking! A cabaret production! This is great, now people will pay to watch a chef cook and they don't even get to eat. Whoever invented this must be in stitches with laughter. Maybe we can have a show on people washing dishes too.

The degustation is a great concept and I'm not going to sit here and say the whole thing is a load of rubbish, but too much of a good thing can be a drawback. When we start to get around ten courses or even more, each with its own wine, we start to get into the realm of just tasting and not eating.

Three bites and the dish is gone; two sips of wine and it's gone, time for the next one. That smoked John Dory, burnt potato, mustard and nashi was great, but it was gone in ninety seconds and I didn't get the chance to enjoy it. My compromise is to limit the menu to five or six courses. Each course is a little bigger and each glass a little more full. Dinner is to be enjoyed. You're not a judge in a competition who needs to taste fifteen dishes.

Over time I have become a more experienced diner and a less experienced chef. I would now make a much better restaurant reviewer than I would a chef cooking a modern degustation menu. And after ten years out of the kitchen, I have become an old man in a young man's world.

Chefs are now like sports stars. We have open kitchens where guests can watch the chefs cook, we can visit their website, get their DVD and their cookbooks. We know the chefs by name and how many restaurants they have. We know every detail about the food we eat, where it comes from and how it was cooked.

Where it all goes to next I'm not really sure. When I first heard about Ferran Adrià at elBulli in Spain I, like many others, figured he was just another crazy nut case chef. But as it turned out, he wasn't. So if I couldn't spot this trend, I'm not really much of a judge as to what is next – but I think I can say what is *not* next.

Chapter 8

Nose to tail

I just don't understand the fascination with eating guts and waste products. During my parents' and grandparents' era, offal was a regular part of the diet for any working-class family because it was cheap; management class had the steak and we had the chops, mince, brains and liver.

My father Norm worked for the railways all his life. He was good at it; very good. In fact, when he died in 2005 several old workmates of his made a point of coming to me and telling me stories about him and just how good he was at his job. But despite being very good at his job, this was a time when wages were much lower and the cost of living more expensive than today in relative terms.

It used to be said that the English eat to live and the French live to eat. Which until not long ago was largely true; the meals that I was brought up on were largely there to give sustenance. And to be honest, that was all we knew. Food that we had to eat because that's all we could afford has now become the domain of the fashionable.

Consequently, we ate fairly plain food. That's all there was. We never went to restaurants because we couldn't afford to. Besides, a barbeque and an esky full of beer with mates in the backyard was always more fun. It might descend into backyard cricket or kick-to-kick football in the street. Life was fairly simple and fun and the food matched that lifestyle.

We used dripping on bread instead of butter because butter was too expensive. Foods like bacon, mushrooms, steak, pork and even chicken were treats and only available to us if the budget was in surplus. For the most part, it was rissoles or chops and three veg, stewed plums from the plum tree and ice-cream. The big treat was every second Thursday: on Dad's payday, my brother and I would get a chocolate Freddo Frog

My fondness for history lessons is necessary because my kids simply have no idea that life was so different in times gone by. The thought that we could not afford butter, that mushrooms would be a real treat, that we would never go out to a restaurant and that brains, liver, kidneys and other internal organs would actually be eaten by people not in prison; all this would not occur to my kids in their world of Facebook, twitter and mobile phones.

Over the years we have become so indulged in the choices and variety of food available and the food that we can afford on a regular basis that I, along with most of Australian society, have become spoilt. We are constantly demanding that chefs come up with something new to dazzle and entertain us. Don't give me a 'risotto with spinach, confit of duck and drizzled with truffle oil' again, I've had it or something similar a hundred times before. What's new?

In our quest for the new, some chefs have gone back to the old. Sick of steak, braised duck, lamb loin cooked two ways, taleggio cheese soufflés and smoked beetroot salad with maple dressing and caramelised almonds? Well then, they have something special. The chef has gone to a great deal of effort to give us 'sweetbreads with beurre noisette, pancetta and South Australian capers' or 'parmesan-crumbed lamb's brains with a baby witlof salad and roasted red-pepper rouille' or 'pig's trotters stuffed with prunes and sage'.

This type of food gets a lot of press because it's interesting, but let's be honest. The vast majority of people including myself don't eat this stuff because, well, why would they? It's not 1965. And the truth of the matter is, it just doesn't sell. Given the choice of pork loin or pig's feet, most people choose pork loin. Given the choice of prawns or sweetbreads, what would you choose?

I really do struggle to see the appeal of sweetbread. What are sweetbreads, I hear you say? They sound nice. I like sweet things and I like bread, so to combine the two must be good. This is what happens when the marketing people take a waste product and dress it up for sale as a delicacy. Sweetbread is the pancreas or the thymus gland from the throat of a young animal, usually a calf. The thymus gland helps the immune system in a young animal. Try putting 'crumbed thymus glands' on the menu and see how many you sell.

So, what do sweetbreads taste like? Well, nothing really, they are very mild with not much flavour at all. What do lambs brains taste like? Again, not much, so I wouldn't bother. What's so special about kidneys? Nothing. A kidney spends all its time while in the animal filtering urine. That is why a chef has a lot of soaking and blanching to do just to make it vaguely edible. It can be eaten, but why would you?

For the most part, people are repulsed by the thought of eating much of this so-called food. And there is no flavour reward for eating most of these foods, either. I hate to see waste and my dog does seem very happy with his lot, so I say let Fido have the offal and I'll have the meat. I also wouldn't bother with the following:

- Tripe, or cow's stomach. Yes, the stomach. You can almost feel the slimy pieces of tripe in white sauce sliding down your throat into your own stomach. Come on, surely we are not so poor that we need to have a cow's stomach in our stomach. Put it on the menu, I dare you.
- Ox heart. Ever wondered why you don't see ox heart on the menu very often? There is a very good reason why. Short of starving, why would you even contemplate eating it? Same goes for pig's spleen and pig's intestines – enough said.

- Fish heads. I don't mind when the head is served on a whole fish, but to serve only the head? Yes, the cheeks are tasty, but to get any decent serving size you need about ten heads per person.
- Testicles. Really, you're going to eat balls for dinner? Or worse, in Asian countries: penis. Surely I don't need to explain this one.
- Duck tongue. Often found in Chinese salads; not worth the bother.

Like many other chefs, I am a great fan of the pig. This is a wonderful animal that together with the duck has given me a great deal of culinary pleasure in the past and will continue to do so as long as I am still capable of eating solid food. When I go out to a restaurant, I look for duck and pork on the menu above all else. But there does seem to be a fashion for their waste products that I don't quite understand. I also think it is unnecessary given our relative affluence.

I really can't see even myself out to dinner with my wife and ordering the pig's head for dinner. Imagine this. The waiter comes over, Joanne orders the lamb loin salad and a glass of chardonnay, and I order a pig's head and a bottle of shiraz. Any expectation of sex that night goes right out the window as the words come out my mouth. What self-respecting woman will want to kiss (let alone get romantic with) a man who has just gorged on pig's head or cow's tongue for dinner? Henry VIII got away with it because he was King, but most of us are not the King.

'Ah, but,' I hear you say, 'the great chefs of the world have taken up the nose to tail philosophy with vigor.' Sure, that's true, but this is just another form of masturbation for their own amusement and pleasure. Really, the general public are not that interested. 'What about Fergus?' I can hear you screaming at the pages of the book. Yes, Fergus Henderson is a chef, a real chef and a very good chef. Fergus owns and cooks at St John Bar and Restaurant in London and is the leader of the nose-to-tail approach to cooking. His restaurant specialises in all the guts that I say people don't want. He not only survives, but does extremely well and has a couple of Michelin stars in his back pocket to prove his point. He also goes against my rule of swapping from another profession into cooking later in life. Yes, Fergus is the real thing and by all accounts, his food is very, very good. But in a world with room for one Van Gogh, one Gandhi, one JFK, one Muhammad Ali and one Dalai Lama (well, one at a time, anyway) there is only room for one Fergus and chefs shouldn't try to emulate his feats.

In the world of bizarre food and offal (and eating what may be considered as waste), there are a few diamonds in the bucket of dirty stones. Even the bizarre food test does have some exceptions; one where the flavour pay-off is so good that if somebody said to you that you are eating gorilla buttocks you would say, 'Fine, just pass the plate.' And that is liver. Liver is really, really nice.

Duck liver is the best, but calf and chicken livers are also very good. They are very versatile and have great taste. Not just a bland, nothing flavour like a sweetbread or brains, but real full-on flavour. Duck and chicken livers are, of course, the main ingredient in pâté. Goose liver is sold as the famous foie gras and imported from France as it is not made locally. It's very expensive, rich and very high in fat. It's so good that I would eat it every day if it were not for the fact that I don't have that kind of money and even if I did, I would probably die of a heart attack after thirty days.

Then there's caviar, tiny, salty, fishy eggs of pure pleasure. The good stuff is from Russia or Iran and can be a couple of thousand dollars a kilo. You can also get local salmon caviar that is very good at a fraction of the price as it comes from farmed salmon rather the wild sturgeon. Is it worth it? Yes, yes, yes, it is worth it. Eat and be happy.

And then there is the chef's favorite: bone marrow. You know when you have a piece of osso buco and after eating the meat you are left with the circle of shinbone in the middle? Always take the time to eat the bone marrow; you won't be sorry. Chefs order veal bones, roast them and use them to make a jus (but they always scoop out the marrow for their own little snack before making the jus). It was so good, chefs started roasting the shinbones and placing about four of the marrows on a plate for an entrée with some toast. A typical chef's meal. Eat and enjoy (although it can also give you a heart attack).

Sea urchins are weird looking and smell of the sea. Try putting some fresh sea urchin on your sushi and you will be asking why nobody ever told you about this stuff before. How come hardly anybody knows that this stuff is so good?

Most Australians salivate over a cold beer and a bucket of prawns on a summer day by the beach, even I like that. But in our haste to get to the prawn meat in the tail, we behead the prawn and discard everything but the meat. Unknown to all but a few is that the prawn's head and shell have even more flavour than the meat.

The Japanese slowly grill the whole prawn on the teppanyaki, bathe it in garlic butter, rip off the head, suck the insides out then eat the rest. Often the Chinese don't even bother to peel the prawn, they just split the back, remove the vein, deep fry the whole thing and wok toss in Sichuan chilli. They eat it whole; heads and all. Crispy chilli prawns, mmm.

On the beach in Sri Lanka or Hoi An in Vietnam, whole prawns are battered and sold wrapped in small newspaper cups as snacks, the same way Australians eat potato crisps. They eat them whole; head, shell, everything.

Deep-fried duck beaks. What, duck beaks! Well, yes, I am a bit embarrassed to say that I go to a restaurant just near the palace in Bangkok and always have deep-fried duck beaks. Crispy and a bit like the duck version of pork crackling, they are an excellent snack while drinking cold beer in a hot Asian climate.

Also in the good file are braised veal cheeks, ox tails and black pudding. Made from the blood of a pig, black pudding has a unique flavour and is one of the few bizarre foods on my list of nose-to-tail acceptable foods.

I am very grateful that I am in a position to be the first one in my family to taste food such as caviar, foie gras and sea urchin; but I eat them because they taste good. I am indeed fortunate that I live in a time where I can afford to eat such delicacies but without the big-time flavour pay-off I wouldn't eat these bizarre foods, what's the point? I'd stick to real food: roast duck, T-bone steaks, crayfish salads, braised veal, Irish stew, pork cutlets. Yes, that's right. Real food.

Chapter 9

My life of crime

At some stage in every chef's career you find yourself in the position of being a gun for hire. Sometimes you are waiting for just the right job to come along. At other times you don't really want another cooking job and are just avoiding the responsibility. This has happened to me throughout my career and it was always very reassuring to know that I could at least get some kind of work. Theoretically, I wouldn't starve.

There are many staffing agencies specialising in cooks so agency work is always available. If you can cook and hold your cool then agency work is okay for a while, but I found after about eight weeks or so I would start to go nuts. Agency work puts you in all sorts of situations. If a restaurant is so desperate for a chef that they need to call the services of a staffing agency and accept whoever walks in the door, they are probably really in the shit and you will be able to do nothing more than hold the fort for a day or two. Sometimes even that is not possible. On other occasions, I would be sent to a hospital or nursing home to fill in for somebody on holiday or off sick. Good, simple eight-hours-a-day work. A walk in the park for a cook used to à la carte work.

Pubs can be the worst of all. Sometimes you get sent to a pub that is really in trouble. You walk into the kitchen and the whole place has a stale, beer smell. No-one is around. There might be a note on the bench if you are lucky, but if not, you go searching for a venue manager who often has very little knowledge of and even less interest in the kitchen side of the business. You're already getting concerned as you have been in this situation before and it's not pretty. You find the manager having a smoke in the drinks storeroom out the back. He says to expect about fifteen people for lunch. But you know there is a real chance that forty-five will turn up.

You look in the coolroom and there's a bucket of green liquid. Maybe it's pea soup; maybe its broccoli soup; maybe it's something else. You have a taste. Mmm, still not sure. Best to ignore it and start afresh. I do the same with the seafood that's marinating and the crumbed veal. With visions of newspaper headlines detailing food poisoning, I grab the menu and cross off half the dishes. I look in the fridge and freezer for fresh food that should be safe to serve. These idiots think I'm Jesus and can feed people from scraps and nothing.

I make a quick onion soup and open a tin of demi-glace for sauces and a few packets of portioned steaks. I grab some fish fillets and a 2-kilogram pack of frozen peas from the freezer and cut some carrots. I prepare a tray of sliced potatoes with butter, cream and garlic and at least I have something to serve. There is a chocolate cake, banana cake and some lemon meringue pie in the display cabinet so I resolve to ignore the dessert menu.

I only arrived at 10 am and now it's 11.45. I could get dockets at any time. I take a look at the entrées. Half have been crossed out but there is still garlic prawns, beef satay, frozen calamari rings, soup and a couple of other items. I cut up a couple of steaks for satay sticks and look for the commercially made satay sauce in a jar in the pantry. As I expect, it's there.

Next I look at the mains menu. Steaks are in the fridge along with some chicken fillets. I defrost some fish and make a beer batter. The veal is looking very suspect with a green tinge so the best place for it is in the bin. I boil some pasta and set up the fry station. All okay. Hope nobody comes.

The docket machine starts to click and an order for two steaks with mushroom sauce is printed. That's okay. But the nineteen-year-old waitress seems to be cutting a lot of bread. I ask her why and she says the table of fourteen has just arrived. What table of fourteen? I start to sweat and get a sinking feeling in my body. I am now fully aware that a slamming is about to occur, but as angry as I am I still need to pay my mortgage and put food on the table at home. All my instincts tell me to pick up my knives and sneak out the back door, but I don't. Dockets are printing like mad and I still haven't got the order for the table of fourteen yet. The venue manager is now looking worried as he can see the customers pouring into the dining room. The docket of fourteen arrives and is added to the long queue on the docket rack.

I realise I don't have enough food prepared and that I'm in real trouble, however the dining room seems oblivious to this fact and keeps taking orders. The venue manager attempts to help me but is more of a hindrance than a help. Another docket of four arrives. The venue manager is chatting up the waitress so I screw up the docket and put it in my pocket. It never existed, these people are not getting fed today: I will deny all knowledge and by then it will be too late. The chaos goes on but ends thankfully at 3 pm. I grab a bottle of beer from the coolroom and go out the back in the lane for a drink.

I come back in the kitchen and the venue manager is again flirting with the waitress; I think there's a very good chance he is screwing her. He thanks me for doing such a great job and asks if I can come back for the rest of the week. I inform him that sadly I already have a booking for the next few days (I don't), put the food in the coolroom, give him an invoice and hightail it out of there. Safely out the door I phone the agency and say don't book me with these idiots again. I go home, have a shower and get drunk. Tomorrow is another day.

A week later I have a day off on a Tuesday. At 3 pm I get a phone call from the agency that a pub close to my home wants a chef from 5 pm to 9 pm tonight. Reluctantly I accept: it's four hours' pay. I arrive and walk in the kitchen to find a full-page note on the bench ready with instructions for me. 'Bus arrives at 6.30 pm: fifty-five people.' The note then proceeds to give me a list of fifty-five pre-ordered meals of roasts, porterhouse steaks, fish and chips – all the usual pub menu standard fare. Fuck, fuck, fuck, I've been conned again. At ten minutes past five a happy-go-lucky lady about forty years old walks into the kitchen wearing an apron. Cheryl usually works in the bar but sometimes helps in the kitchen. I move into action and plan the culinary crime that I am about to commit. The small monkey-see monkey-do tasks like making salads and setting up the fry station are delegated to Cheryl. It's just over an hour till the bus arrives. I slice a big tray of potatoes and place in the oven. Next I grab some frozen peas and frozen carrots from the freezer. Using sauces from a tin and packets of food from the coolroom, there is no actual cooking involved. The idea is to get something on a plate, anything, it doesn't even have to taste good, as long as it fills them up. It may as well be soylent green for all anybody cares.

Somehow we manage to get most of it together by 7 pm. The customers arrive at 6.30 pm but we are not ready so they have a couple of drinks first. We bang the so-called food on plates and send them out via a couple of so-called waiters. We heave a sigh of relief. Thank god, that's over. The kitchen looks like a bomb's hit it, everything is everywhere. In this situation you don't care how much mess you make. Cheryl gets me a beer and we start to clean down. At 9 pm I give my invoice to Cheryl and get the hell out of there.

You see, there are food pubs and beer pubs. This is a beer pub and as such the only thing that counts is the number of beer barrels sold at the end of the week. Everything else is a side issue. The pub is probably even owned by a beer company as a venue to sell their product. The kitchen is just a necessary evil and is really only there because it has to be.

During this time I worked in various hospitals, sometimes for a day, sometimes for two weeks or more. Once they got to know you they would ask the agency for you in particular. One place stands out. It was a large, suburban, public hospital and I worked there quite a bit on a semi-regular basis. It was a 7.6-hour shift with 45 minutes for lunch but the cooks there had no real intention of cooking; they were on a gravy train and were enjoying the ride.

What was happening in fact was fraud on a grand scale. The kitchen was well maintained and clean but unlike other hospitals where I had worked – where there was an emphasis on fresh, healthy nutritious food – the aim was to do as little actual cooking as possible. For example, a soup would need to be made every day. Their version of asparagus soup entailed filling a kettle with about 30 litres of water, mixing in the appropriate amount of powdered asparagus soup from 2 kilogram tins to the right thickness, adding a couple of tins of asparagus cuts and bringing to the boil, then finishing by adding a dash of cream. Cream of celery or tomato soup was made in a similar way. Vegetable soup was made the same way with the addition of frozen peas and corn.

Most of the soup menu was like this. Once I noticed pumpkin soup was on the menu and, knowing that there were no pumpkin soup tins in the pantry and that there was a 10 kilogram bag of cut pumpkin pieces in the coolroom, I began making a real pumpkin soup. I was quickly pulled up by the chef who saw me peeling onions. I was instructed to use the powdered onion in the pantry in the convenient chef's pack of two-kilo tins. I was totally shocked, ashamed and disgusted all at the same time. The most basic first-year apprentice task of a pumpkin soup had been turned into a lazy mix and serve of flavoured water.

I wasn't surprised when I found that mash potato came in 5-kilogram boxes of potato flakes. Mixed every day and served without embarrassment, there were frozen peas and frozen beans for vegetables. Mains were not really much better: bulk tortellini pasta with a sauce from crushed tomato tins; roast meat cooked the day before, sliced cold and reheated in the steamer, it looked and tasted like cardboard. Cheap, frozen fish pieces were run through the oven and topped with a fake sauce of some kind, maybe hollandaise from a tetra pack. Desserts were dishes like apple crumble (from a tin), cream caramel (from a packet), jelly (from a packet), apple pie (frozen).

The main task of the cooks in this kitchen seemed to be reading the newspaper. The 15-minute morning coffee break was extended to 30 minutes. The 45-minute lunch break blew out to one and a half hours and the afternoon 15-minute break was extended to 30 minutes again. In a 7.6-hour shift, these guys did little more than 5 hours' work. They liked me because I went with the flow: I wasn't there to change the world, I was there to pay my mortgage.

I came home one night and made Joanne and my eldest daughter promise me that if I was ever in hospital they would bring me in a restaurant-standard meal every evening for dinner just like Arthur did for his dying valet Hobson in the 1981 film, *Arthur*.

I knew that someone would have to see this situation for what it really was and was relieved when one day the hospital was talking about contracting out the catering services. The kitchen staff went on strike to protect their jobs and a major drama ensued, the union was on the nightly news saying that these poor cooks were worried about losing their jobs. They had good reason to worry and in the end they were all kicked off the gravy train.

Another regular job was in the banquet department of a top five-star hotel. Often there would be four or five agency cooks there at one time with just two or three of their own staff. The hours were enormous and the agency guys were making a lot of money; they were getting paid about two or three times the wages of the hotel staff. This of course created resentment from the hotel cooks and there was always a steady tension in the kitchen. The chef de cuisine never did any real work and the sous chef just barked orders at some poor English chef de partie who was stuck on a two-year contract. Doing agency work was okay because you got paid by the hour but the word in the industry was don't take a job there.

Despite this poor management and the lack of any real kitchen brigade the food that was being produced was of a very high standard. and I learnt a lot about high quality big production cooking They would attempt menu items that I thought would fail but they didn't. In the public eye they had a great reputation because the food was very good. It may have been a five-star property but behind the scenes it was chaos.

Being a travelling minstrel also puts you in contact with the fruitcakes and nutcases of the industry and the question arises as to when to walk out and leave people to fend for themselves. I only ever did this once. It was Valentine's Day so every restaurant was full and everybody wanted another chef, another a pair of hands, anybody. I was booked in to start at 4 pm. I had already done a shift at a nursing home in the morning but doubled up for an evening shift as well.

I arrived and introduced myself to the manager and he sent me to the kitchen. I got changed and grabbed my knife box to start work, I walked past another cook there and for some reason he deliberately bumped into me; it was plainly deliberate. Confused by the action I apologised but he still went absolutely nuts; called me everything under the sun. His eyes glazed over and I sensed real danger. The whole situation just didn't make sense.

Was he a space cadet? Had his wife just left him? Was he just a guy who had worked too many hours for too little pay and had expected to be in a better position at thirty? Who knows! Looking around the kitchen I could see nobody was coming to sort out the situation and I thought it would be a really long night; they already looked under pressure and were struggling to get the mis en place ready. I could see all the ingredients of a major disaster, the recipe was in motion and I had a feeling of déjà vu. I noted that my knife box and bag were on the way out and easy to get to without the need to carry them past the other chef so with my heart thudding anxiously in my chest, I headed for the door. At the front door, the manager asked, 'Where are you going?'

'Home,' I said and got out of there as fast as I could, before they all went nuts. Chalking it up to experience, I went home, had a shower and got drunk. Tomorrow was another day.

Of course, agency work is not always like this. My time as a hired gun was about half and half a life of crime versus honest cooking. There are nursing homes out there making fresh scones for morning tea and healthy, nutritious, real food every day for lunch and dinner (some even have a bar trolley that goes around serving beer and wine to the residents). There are cafes out there doing great cafe food for busy customers who need a meal on the run. Sometimes it's easy and sometimes you get ambushed on the battlefield: you never really know until you get there.

Chapter 10

Getting out

Some people become chefs because they have a passion for cooking. Others just fall into the job. Either way, life often doesn't turn out exactly the way you expect. For many chefs who started cooking in their late teens and are now over thirty-five a mid-life crisis is both common and normal. I would go as far as to say that almost all chefs over forty are looking for a way out: a way to live a normal life taking your son to football or your daughter to netball; going to your nephew's wedding on a Saturday; attending the kids' school play on a Wednesday night; or having dinner with your wife.

After a career of cooking, most chefs are in the same position with a mortgage, a car loan and two kids at school. You're finally at a stage where you're earning good money. Sure, you have to work 65 hours a week, but it pays the bills. But as a chef, you are always the family member who is missing. Kids are great, they seem to take it all in their stride, but you know they are missing out on a lot.

How can you go home to your partner and say, 'I've lost the passion and want to stop cooking.' You feel like you're stuck in *Groundhog Day*; each day is the same with no way out. It's all well and good to have the love and support of your wife or husband but it doesn't pay the mortgage. What other job could you step into that pays as good as what you are on now? What else do you have the skills to do?

This was my situation along with a thousand others. My options had started to dry up. I had tried a catering business, tried the corporate chef world, tried the hotels, done agency work and the opportunity for a rock star existence had long since withered on the vine. Many chefs in this situation buy their own restaurant but with a slow economy and having been burnt once already in business, I didn't want to risk our house on an all-or-nothing gamble of restaurant ownership. A gamble that statistically ends in tears.

Old chefs in general are sad chefs; you can see it in their eyes. There's defeat in the lines on their face and in the scars on their hands. This is what I was most afraid of: regret. A destructive emotion that wastes your life, regret renders you unable to change the past while feeling locked into a future chosen by somebody else. Taking control is hard and requires a long-term plan.

I meet chefs all the time, they're everywhere. They're truck drivers, taxi drivers, real-estate agents, salesmen, equipment guys, TAFE teachers, construction workers, food-safety consultants, mining workers – they are ABC (anything but cooking); chefs who have managed to get out. Have a beer with a forty-two-year-old chef and he will ask you if you have any jobs going: teaching, sales, whatever you have or know is available.

I had a TV antenna installed at my home the other day by a guy who had been a chef of eighteen years. He had worked all around the world. A Hyatt man like me, he had owned two restaurants and had two broken marriages behind him. He was working as a pastry chef at a three Michelin star restaurant in London for £450 a week when a friend who worked in the building industry offered him a labourer's job on a building site for £800 a week. He never cooked again. Now he installs TV antennas and is as happy as Larry; he has a life again.

Most chefs don't get out. As much as they would like to start a new way of life, they are addicted to the one they already have: the camaraderie in the kitchen; the sense of pride that comes from cooking nice food that people enjoy; and the adrenalin rush you get from service.

You might think by reading this book that cooking is not a career I would recommend to young people. You'd be wrong. Cooking is a tremendously satisfying job. One where you really can see, taste and enjoy the work that you do – and if you do a good job, other people fawn and fuss over you, thanking you for the great meal that made their day, night, evening. You also get the chance to understand and enjoy good food and good wine. I have always thought that whether you are rich or poor, if you can eat well throughout your life, you should die happy.

Being a chef makes you part of our own unique subculture within hospitality. Chefs all around the world feel a sense of kinship with each other, an unwritten respect because you know what they have been through and what they are capable of. Watching another chef work in the kitchen during service, seeing them add ingredients and cook meals is truly a thing of beauty. And if I am in a restaurant with an open kitchen, I find it hard not to watch and admire.

Chefs have their own language, their own terms. Only another chef can really understand the stories they tell when drinking beer at 1 am on a Thursday night at a chef's bar – a bar that stays open late to get the trade of the hospitality workers as they knock off. It's really cool to be part of this group; to be one of the elite who can not only do the job, but do it well.

You see, once you are a chef you will always be a chef. Even if you become a sales rep or a truck driver, in your mind you are still a chef. To the other cooks and chefs who fought the hard battles with you, you are still a chef. Colleagues you meet again after years and years will still call you chef.

Once you have been a chef, your mode of thinking changes, the way you work changes and your attitude changes. You still think like a chef no matter what else you do. It's our own private club – and membership is paid in aches, pains, cuts, burns, blood, tears, arguments and time; above all, time.

Despite a real love for the job and the lifestyle, the pressure at home to do something else is great. It wears you down drop by drop, cut by cut, day by day. After almost twenty years, it can all get too much. I love being a chef – I hate being a chef!

The problem is real and a very difficult one to solve. Most chefs don't really have any other skills than cooking and managing a kitchen. This is an awesome skill that not everybody has, but it is very specific and unfortunately, doesn't always set you up for much else. In fact, I just attended the Fine Food Australia trade show in Melbourne and saw many cooks and chefs that I hadn't seen in years. Some were still cooking, but most weren't and had gone on to a variety of positions within related industries. The obvious alternatives are sales reps for food companies or a cooking teacher in TAFE.

If you want to get out, there are numerous obstacles in your way. The sales reps and good teaching jobs are hard to get and very competitive and you'll need an edge to get in like a really good relationship with the supplier or having a mate who is already teaching. There is also the problem of a lack of education and training if you want to get out of the food industry altogether. It is very hard to enrol in a TAFE course to learn a new skill working the hours and times that chefs do. Starting over also means you have to start at the bottom again, meaning a large drop in salary: one you probably can't afford to take.

The possibility of it taking three years just to catch up again is very frustrating for middle-aged, tired, jaded chefs who just want a day off to go to the football with the kids or catch some quality time with their partner at night.

For some chefs, change is forced upon them: after about fifteen years a chef's body starts to give way. The knees are probably one of the earliest to go. Chefs continually bend over and kneel down to use the ovens, get plates from the floor-level hot press and shift supplies, Hips are the next to go for similar reasons. Tall chefs face particular problems; with a standard bench height of 900 mm, they spend most of their time crouched over, completely wrecking their lower back muscles. And standing all day, every day, on a hard, tiled, kitchen floor, also causes back pain that only gets worse over the years. It becomes a life of paracetamol, ibuprofen and Voltaren. After fifteen or twenty years, it's no wonder they need to move onto something else.

Manual-handling injuries are the most common occupational health and safety problem in Australia and the hospitality industry has its fair share of these injuries. Chefs are always lifting and carrying stores of food. Young chefs think they are invincible but one simple act of lifting a carton the wrong way can ruin your back completely; it can't be fixed and you can no longer work in a kitchen.

In general, the only sectors of the hospitality industry that take occupational health and safety (OH&S) seriously are the big hotels, casinos and the large franchise operations. Cafes, restaurants and even most pubs often know very little about OH&S and the aggressive culture of chefs who think nothing matters except getting the mis en place done and being there for service puts themselves at risk. Major cut or burn? Patch it up and get back to work.

I knew I had to get out but teaching osso buco to a class of twenty apprentices didn't thrill me either. I am my own worst enemy; never content, I don't want to do this and don't want to do that. Having seen others live life, eat in restaurants and travel overseas, I was no longer happy just existing. It's a blessing and a curse.

Not all chefs are like this, however. Anyone who has spent time standing at the stove with an Asian chef knows that they have a very different attitude to life and very different expectations to those raised in Australia or Europe. In general, Asians are not slaves to the big pay packet or the promotion; they don't feel as though they have to be the boss like Anglo-Saxons, Americans or Europeans do. If a job provides income, interest, some enjoyment and camaraderie, then in general, they don't really want for much more.

Europeans, on the other hand, tend to define their identity by their job, their social status, their income and the recognition they obtain from it. Western European culture worships the individual and competition whereas the Asian Hindu/Buddhist culture is one where happiness, contentment and peace comes from within – not from your workplace or your achievements.

Most Asian chefs are generally happy being chefs and want to cook for their whole life. They are contented people. I know Indian chefs who have worked at the tandoori oven cooking naan and tandoori chicken their whole life, Chinese chefs who have never done anything else except make dim sum, Japanese chefs who do nothing but sushi. From a western perspective you would think they would get bored and want to move on, change jobs, but they don't. If a restaurateur treats them well and pays them properly they will stay loyal employees forever. They rarely take days off, they rarely complain, their skill is unchallenged and they are really nice guys. I look at them with envy but don't know how to become one of them.

I knew I was caught up in a merry go round and wanted to get off, but didn't know how. I went to Crown with the explicit purpose of getting out, and after more training and education there I felt I was in a position to make the move. The dream was a nine-to-five, Monday to Friday job and a Ford Falcon. In essence, I wanted to be my father.

But there were roadblocks everywhere I turned. I was either not qualified or not quite what people were looking for. I even thought product development at Pizza Hut sounded like a good job at the time so I took Joanne and the kids there for dinner just to have a look. I thought as a chef I could make some real changes here and make a difference. I was excited and sent off the application. Thanks, but no thanks, came the reply. There was another opportunity for a corporate chef with a smorgasbord chain of restaurants. Again I had a look and figured I could make some improvements so sent off the application only to find out the whole company went into receivership two weeks later. Applications for sales jobs at grocery companies followed and failed. Jobs that actually suited me were few and far between. Jobs that I actually had any interest in were even fewer.

I did go for one job that was advertised as 'food development'. Not knowing what that meant but becoming increasingly desperate, I applied. It turned out to be a consultancy and training group specialising in food that was part of a TAFE college. Despite having a team of about fifteen staff, they didn't have a chef on board so I told them straight that this was crazy and that they should hire me straight away. They admired my forthrightness, but I clearly didn't really fit into their organisation. The boss liked me though and offered me $5 000 to write a food safety program for a restaurant. I wasn't really sure how to do such a thing but I readily accepted the $5 000.

I stayed at Crown until I took a redundancy and continued to work on the food safety program, hoping that it would become permanent but it didn't. My only option left was to create my own job, a tried and true route for many chefs in my situation. Along the way I had discovered an important lesson that would ultimately help me: if it is written on a business card, it is without question true. So I had cards printed that said, 'Phillip McMillan – chef, food consultant, trainer'. This helped a great deal: it was all a bluff, but people took me more seriously with a business card.

Chapter 11

Rock stars and bamboo

Apart from a total career change or gradual metamorphosis from chef to some other food related occupation, there are two other ways out. They may be not available to everybody and or even to everyone's taste but for a selected or brave few they are on the menu of life. One is to become a rock star and the other is to 'go bamboo'.

The rock star chef, well what can I say? They still cook but don't do the mis en place day after day, week after week, month after month and year after year. These guys live the dream. People go to their restaurants like they are going to an Elton John concert. We see them on the red carpet at theatre openings, their photos are in the social pages on a Sunday and they host lavish charity events. Such a beast never existed when I was cooking. Sure, a few chefs had daytime spots on the midday show but they weren't stars; we were drunks, not stars.

The rock star chef has become a brand, and a brand is a very valuable commodity in the twenty-first century. Some have restaurants all over the world, others have a chain over Australia or just two or three in their home town. You know who they are and you know their names.

We all see the rock stars and think we can do it too; it looks easy. But if every kid who picked up a guitar and practised Deep Purple's 'Smoke on the Water' became a rock star, they would no longer be special. If every kid like me picked up a pan and became a rock star chef we would all have a TV show, three cookbooks and be a consultant to Qantas. There is by the very nature of the system a limited number of rock star chef places available. Yes, it's possible to become a rock star … but unlikely.

The other way out is to 'go bamboo'. It was Anthony Bourdain – an accidental rock star who achieved the dream or getting out of the kitchen by becoming a great writer and TV personality – who first introduced me to the term gone bamboo. It's a term that was used to describe World War II soldiers from western countries who didn't go home to their family, their dog, their wife or their suburban jobs; they stayed in Asia and lived a new lifestyle and new life. They had gone bamboo.

In February 2011, I am sitting on a small plastic chair at the side of the road in Phan Thiet, Vietnam. There are about eight of us, and we are at a small, local seafood restaurant in the wharf area of this fishing town. The Tiger Beer maids in sexy blue satin dresses keep us full of beer and plates of seafood seem to just arrive in front of us. As we order more food, a little twelve-year-old boy runs across the road to one of the fishing boats on the dock just 30 metres away. He scurries back with a small bucket of large prawns. Five minutes later, the prawns are on our table. It's all good, very good in fact.

Of my friends at the table, Les, Carl, Dan and Niall have all gone bamboo, never to return home. Each story is different, but the same. They came to Vietnam on business, returned for a closer look – and vowed never to return home. Wives, kids, houses, cars, jobs; none of it mattered any more; they had been engulfed by a foreign culture and a much simpler more decadent lifestyle.

Les now teaches and runs a school in Saigon. Carl runs a kite-surfing shop in Mui Ne. Dan owns a farm growing dragon fruit and after six months of hedonistic pursuit, Niall has just run out of money and is looking for work as an English teacher.

We eat and drink all night, throwing our empty bottles and food scraps under the table (that's how it is done there.) The bill is about $100 for eight people. These guys do this all the time, following the advice of Timothy Leary: turn on, tune in, drop out. They drift from bar to bar, girl to girl, and restaurant to restaurant. Their iPods are full of Eric Burdon, The Doors and Creedence Clearwater Revival blasting into their heads while they disappear for twenty minutes at a time with a bar prostitute who has long legs, a short skirt and a smiley face tattoo on her arse. No, they're not going home!

When I worked in hotels, I noticed a peculiar trait among the nomad upper-management chefs. Many were German and Swiss, but their wives were Asian. I didn't think much of it at the time, but now when I look at their lifestyle, and having travelled to many parts of Asia myself, I can see why. These chefs are international citizens of the world: two years at the Hyatt Tokyo; two years at the London Hilton; four years at the Dubai Marriott; one year at Raffles Singapore. Their life goes on like this forever and European, Australian and American women simply would not put up with the constant uprooting and shifting to a new country.

Chefs get posted all over the world, but when they get posted to Asia – and especially places like Bali, Thailand, Vietnam or some fantasy resort in Penang – they change. Even big cities like Saigon, Bangkok or Jakarta change a person. All of a sudden a cocktail of great, cheap food, less responsibility (because most people you know are back in Australia), seventy cent beers pulled from buckets of ice by sexy beer maids, the beauty of the country and the friendliness of the people and many ask the question, 'Why go home? What is there for me besides traffic, a mortgage and complaining relatives? No, I'm not going back and nobody can make me.'

And indeed, many don't: they fuck and drink themselves silly for three years then settle down with a nice, young, caring, Asian girlfriend. They have gone bamboo, never to return. They are still cooking but they no longer care. They live for today, get drunk, eat grilled prawns on the beach and have an unlimited supply of women. If they die tomorrow, that is okay with them because today, they live like Caligula.

Asia is like Hotel California; you can check out any time but you can never leave. However, there is a price to pay for this lifestyle: you must be prepared to leave everything behind in Australia. You can't take any baggage with you when you go bamboo. I didn't go bamboo but I understand the appeal!

Chapter 12

Old-bastard-chef syndrome

For those chefs who don't manage to get out, go bamboo or become a rock star, there is a very real chance they will fall victim to old-bastard-chef syndrome. Some old chefs become bitter and so hard to work for: nothing is ever good enough, everything is always wrong. These guys work hard, very hard. They always work more hours than everybody else and because they have no delegation skills, even when they do try to delegate even simple tasks to other cooks and chefs it never works. It's usually their fault, but in their mind, everybody else is an idiot and they stand as a bastion of hard work and common sense.

I could see this happening to me. The intensity of the whole cooking thing just grinds away at you and can turn even a good man into an old bastard. The current generation of old bastards has no computer skills, resists any form of technology having only just recently bowed to public pressure and got a mobile phone (it's rarely on though). All things can be solved by hard work and long hours. They are the religious martyrs and suicide bombers of the kitchen. Everywhere they go they cause unrest and havoc.

They do have good resumes however and are well spoken so they always get jobs. Some are very well known and highly respected chefs, but behind the facade they are angry and frustrated men lost in time and most cooks will not work for them. So what makes a perfectly reasonable person, a talented chef even, become an old bastard?

To really know why, you must understand that chefs, for the most part, are socially isolated people. Locked in the back of a kitchen, away from the public, they really only associate with the fish deliveryman, other cooks and waiters. The deliveryman is considered a worker bee – necessary, but expendable and easily replaced. He does bring you fish though, so he is treated with respect to his face but still these old bastards feel essentially superior. Younger cooks are also stupid because their generation is full of soft, spoilt, impatient, marijuana-smoking, Facebook fiends who can't cook real food anyway. Obsessed with their hatred for foams, blast chillers, coriander, fish sauce, chilli and the new fashions in cooking, they long for the days of flathead fillets in beurre noisette, beef à la mode and trout almondine.

In the world of the old bastard chef, waiters are considered ill-educated, plate-carrying monkeys who are plotting against you during their pre-service meeting. Treating them like the fools they are is a God-given right of a chef.

Chefs don't really get to associate with many other people. They don't get to go to the football, they don't get to go to the movies, they don't go fishing, they don't belong to a club – they are locked in the kitchen for most of their lives because of the long hours they work.

Some old bastards listen to talkback radio in the kitchen, day in, day out. If you listen to talkback radio for too long anyone will become an old bastard: it's full of how the politicians are wasting our money, judges are letting rapists and murderers off with three years, the public transport system is stuffed, the economy is going down and Telstra is ripping us off again. The long hours stuck in the kitchen listening to this can make a chef paranoid and with the paranoia comes the old-bastard-chefs syndrome. I'd seen this happen to others and was well aware it could happen to me. For despite my dislike of politics, I am fascinated by the ins and outs, the failures and the waste. I often listen to talkback radio despite knowing that it does little other than make be a grumpy old man.

One very well-known and respected chef in Melbourne is the classic old bastard chef. Let's call him Niccolo for argument's sake. Niccolo cooks for sure. He has even achieved great things. Do a google search on him and you'll find heaps; do a google search on me and you will find almost nothing. I cannot deny the achievements of the man. I know how hard the life of a chef can be. He has not only survived but prospered, and deserves respect. That's why it hurts me so much to say he is a miserable old bastard. But a life of social exclusion and dedication to one task and one task only, to serve good food every day to every customer, can do that to a man.

To these guys, it becomes all about the plate: if it's not on the plate it doesn't matter. If they have to yell at you to get the meal exactly how they want it, they do. If the waiter is just a few seconds slow they yell again, the glorious plate is deteriorating, hurry up. Hurry up! They do this day after day after day. They never go to the art gallery, they never go to the tennis – they have no friends to go out with. They have lots of business acquaintances, but very few friends. They kid themselves that they do go out but in reality, when they do have a day off they go to another restaurant for dinner. Their mind is still working, looking at the food, doing a mental food costing and looking for new ideas.

They are the old-school types of chef. The ones who yell, scream, intimidate, belittle and abuse you until you break and scream at them to go get fucked. Only then do they have some respect for you. They would still yell, scream and abuse you, but at least there was a begrudging level of respect established. Of course, if you didn't tell them to get fucked, then you were just a weak, girly, pansy who shouldn't be in the kitchen according to them anyway so the abuse was justified.

Many well-respected and talented chefs, unfortunately well and truly past their best, suffer from old-bastard-chef syndrome. I was once sent to work with Niccolo by the agency. After so long in the industry and hearing so many Niccolo stories, I was eager to meet him. I agreed to the posting out of curiosity and a sense of duty. But when I arrived at the kitchen of his latest restaurant, it was empty. I looked around and eventually Niccolo came out of a back office. Not in chef's whites yet, he said hello, barely looking at me. He showed me the coolroom and gave me a menu, a scribbled mis en place list and disappeared. I started work on the prep.

Half an hour later Niccolo appeared in his whites. He looked old and tired; his eyes showed the lights were on, but nobody was really home. I wondered why he was still doing this. Surely he had made enough money from his restaurants over the years to give this away by now. He proceeded to show me what I had done wrong so far and exactly how he wanted the other tasks to be completed. I quietly complied. I worked and watched, watched and worked.

When a middle-aged woman came in (I assumed she was a manager of sorts) she didn't even have time to settle in before Niccolo started railing at her. However, she wasn't fazed and it all seemed routine to her. All the time Niccolo watched me like a hawk but he didn't talk much and I could see he was not really interested in me at all. The food was important but people weren't.

Niccolo was meticulous with the food and acted like he was still doing fine dining but those days were behind him. Time, the industry and society had moved on and left him in 1983. I boned thirty quails and stuffed them with duxelle, a dish straight out of the classical era.

I did get through my two weeks with Niccolo. It wasn't so much the arguments with various staff that made it difficult, it was more his constant complaining about everything that really dragged me down. The fish was wrong, I didn't do that right, the dockets were written incorrectly, the government was destroying the hospitality industry, it never used to be like this – on and on and on, every day, non-stop. He didn't look happy; he never looked happy. Then why was he still in the kitchen? Because he knows nothing else, that's why!

Chapter 13

Taste and satisfaction

'The point is, ladies and gentleman, that taste, for lack of a better word, is good. Taste is right, taste works. Taste clarifies, cuts through, and captures the essence of the evolutionary spirit. Taste, in all of its forms: taste for life, for money, for love, for knowledge has marked the upward surge of mankind. What's worth doing is worth doing for taste.'

If Gordon Gekko was a chef he might have said that, but he worshiped at the altar of money instead of at the altar of the plate. Taste is the measurement of success. It's what people talk about, what they crave and what they are addicted to. Without it, you have nothing. Why do we like butter, roast pork, strawberries, barbequed onions, lamb sausages and Chinese roast duck? Because they taste good, that's why!

Having come from a background where taste was secondary and not a major consideration for a family meal, to one where I have a greater understanding of cooking and taste, I can never go back. I will not be denied. I do things for taste: I eat for taste, I dream in taste, I crave it and anticipate each parcel of it coming my way. But taste is greatly misunderstood.

Chefs are the high priests of taste. We have it and everybody else wants it. It still seems to amaze me a bit because cooking is not really that hard; it's quite simple really. With a little application almost anyone could become a self-sufficient flavour junkie. But you do need to understand what flavour is, why food tastes good, what flavours are good and what flavours are bad. A short study of the subject from a chef's point of view will help. I will also let you in on some standard tricks of the trade, so you know just how chefs capture that elusive, to-die-for taste that you can never seem to replicate at home.

The first lesson is, fat tastes good. We try not to like it, but we just can't help it. When you sit down to Christmas dinner what do you look forward to? The crackling on the pork? Me too! It's essentially fat. In fact, we are hard-wired to like fat. That's because it has another advantage: it's extremely satisfying. Start the day with a fry-up of eggs, bacon, sausages and toast laden with butter and you will start the day with a smile on your face and satisfaction in your stomach. Finish the day with a deep-fried chicken parmigiana and chips and your brain will be telling you that all is good and right in the world.

Our brain wants us to be fat so we can survive the harsh winter without much food. If hunting is very poor and the woolly mammoth are hard to catch, we need a reserve of fat to serve as nutrition so we don't starve. The Chilean miners who spent sixty-nine days trapped underground lost about 12 or 13 kilograms each. (Kate Moss would have died after fourteen days.) They needed their fat stores in order to survive. But for almost everyone else, fat does little more than raise our blood pressure, clog our arteries, slow us down, make airline seats too small and give us heart disease.

But the instinct and the cravings remain. Adding fat is a cheap and common way to make people satisfied with a meal, but it does taste good. I know, I've done it.

Cream of pumpkin soup, cream of mushroom soup, cream of asparagus soup, cream of cauliflower soup and cream of potato and leek soup. We finish soups with cream to add fat. This lubricates, gives the soup a rich, smooth texture and brings out the flavour of the original ingredients. Try making one of these soups and finish half with cream, leaving the other half plain, and you will see and taste the difference. It is enormous.

Adding fat, though, does not mean heaping everything with cheese. Generally, adding cheese is a lazy way to add fat: cheese on a burger, cheese on a taco, cheese on pizza, cheese on nachos, cheese on a parma. Adding cheese to everything is like cheating really. Take a look at most takeaway foods and you will see that if they are not deep fried, they are loaded with cheese. It's not nice quality, complex-flavoured cheese either: it will be the cheapest, plastic, mass-produced stuff that ever paraded itself as food. It will clog your arteries, slow you down, give you high blood pressure and eventually an early grave. It's tremendously gratifying though because that's what our body wants, what we crave and what we are addicted to: fat, salt and sugar appeal to our most primitive need in terms of nutrition.

We love chips for a number of similar reasons. Most chips are now cooked in flavourless vegetable oils, but in the old days, people cooked them in dripping (which tasted much better). Again, it is the high fat content that makes chips extremely satisfying. Next are the sugars. The starch sugars on the outside of the chip caramelise when we cook them. This is one of our all-time favourite flavours. Chefs know how to make this flavour and they use it in everything to make their food taste good. And finally, we sprinkle it generously with salt. And we all love salt. In a nutshell, these flavours (fat, caramelised sugar and salt) cross over cultures and appeal to our basic instincts. Combined with the cheapness of a potato, it explains the popularity of chips.

Complex flavours such as wine, washed-rind cheeses, coffee, beer, vinegar, chilli, curry and bitter lettuce do not appeal to these basic caveman instincts and so require a more open mind to enjoy. Relax and really taste these foods, and you will see they can be the joy of living. Because these flavours do not have the instant appeal of, say, a donut, the flavours are often mistaken and result in comments such as 'I don't like that,' or 'I hate blue cheese' or 'I can only drink coffee with six sugars'.

This, however, is a trick of your mind. We associate flavours and smells with events in our life. Fat, salt and sugar bring about pleasant, satisfied feelings in our body, because a million years ago, food was scarce: in order to survive, we needed to stock up on these requirements when available.

When we taste a food for the first time, our mind looks for an association. It remembers taste, so when you eat a pineapple for the first time, your mind says, 'Ah, sugar, I love that!' Eat chips for the first time and your mind says, 'Ah, fat, sugar and salt, we really, *really* love that!' Have coffee for the first time without sugar and your mind says, 'What the hell is this! Why am I drinking this?' Sometimes, this is interpreted as 'I don't like coffee' but it is, in fact, 'What is this? I don't understand!' If you relax, take your time and have an open mind, there are in fact very few flavours that are not pleasant. Wine is complex and immensely pleasurable, as is cheese, coffee, vinegar and other foods that do not instantly appear 'nice'.

You will notice that obese people tend to eat more of the foods that appeal to their primitive cravings, and less of the foods that appeal to a more complex palate.

You've just spent $120 on a nine-course degustation menu at that chef from TV's restaurant, and another $100 for the wine package. It was good, very good. Each dish was finely crafted to include the best of ingredients in a way that delights and entertains. You finish the meal with dessert of 'fresh and dried berries intermingled with black olives, an earthy beetroot sorbet and sugar-frosted rose petals' and an espresso coffee. You fork out a wad of crisp, clean $100 notes and you are in the taxi on the way home.

You are feeling pretty happy about yourself, flirting with your partner in the back seat until you see a sign advertising the big yellow arches, a familiar sign to everyone. This sign appeals to your most basic primitive caveman instincts. You don't want it to, though, because doing so would admit to yourself that you have either been conned or, really, are just a normal person after all. However, like a drug addict, you cannot help it and tell the taxi driver to pull over. You wind down the window and order two hamburger meals to go, otherwise your partner will steal yours. You feel a deep shame, but at least you are satisfied.

So were you conned? Were you ripped off? No, not really. You see, the food you got at the restaurant was made with the best of ingredients and is highly labour intensive. To make food like that you need an army of well-paid chefs and an army of poorly paid slave cooks to fuss and stress over every fine detail. That costs a lot of money. Then you need well-paid waiters, ones that really do know what the food is and can explain and understand the intricacies of each dish. Finally, you need a really well-paid sommelier to select, store and serve the wine. All put together like a Mozart symphony, you are as much buying the entrainment value as the food.

So why are you still hungry? You are still hungry because this type food concentrates on flavour, taste and texture, rather than fat, salt and sugar. It's not lazy, deep-fried food topped with plastic cheese. It is lower in fat and has concentrated flavours in portions that are designed to allow you to enjoy the nine courses without throwing up after the fourth course. A hamburger may be more satisfying to the Neanderthal in you but the degustation menu with matching wines is still worth the effort for the experience alone.

Let's now look at some flavours a chef will rely on in cooking.

This is the big one: caramel. Chefs use this flavour in almost everything. Most foods contain natural sugars and starches to some degree. When heat is applied to these natural sugars and starches, the sugars turn to caramel or are browned.

When we cook a steak, it is important to seal it on the grill. This allows good browning of the steak and not only helps to keep the meat tender, but caramelises the sugars on the outside. This is what makes it taste great. To illustrate my point, cook a steak on a very low heat without much browning at all. The steak will not only be tough, it will not have the taste that the browned steak has. You can do the same with onions on a barbeque; cook some on low heat and some browned on high heat. The browned ones taste much, much better.

This basic cooking method forms the basis of a jus. Just brown some beef bones and meat scraps, add some mirepoix (diced onion, celery and carrot) and brown too. Then add some good quality stock, some browned roasting juice and you have the basis of a good jus. Basically, what you have done is built on the flavours made from the principle of caramelising the sugar found in food, in this case, the beef.

We brown everything: chips, chicken, deep-fried items, pastry, toast, fish etc. If you know how to make this flavour, you are well on the way to understanding cooking.

Next is wine. Adding red wine to a jus sounds great; the richness of the red wine goes perfectly with the jus. But we want only the flavour of the wine in the sauce, not the alcohol as, believe it or not, the alcohol will give the sauce an unpleasant flavour. I know it goes against the principle to drink as much red wine as possible for medical purposes, but trust me on this one, the alcohol gives the sauce an unpleasant, raw taste.

So, to turn a jus into a red wine jus, we must first have a brunoise of onions (basically, finely chopped onions). Heat a little oil or butter in a pan, add the onions and cook until they just start to go brown. Now add the wine. Science lesson alert! Alcohol boils at 80°C and water boils at 100°C, so the first steam to come off is the alcohol, not the water. Once the alcohol has evaporated, then you can add the jus. It's the same for any sauce. If you add the wine at the end, the alcohol will stay in the sauce and it will be unpleasant.

You've probably heard that you must use good wine for cooking, the better the wine the better the sauce, the better the coq au vin the better the beef bourguignon. Well does that stand to reason? Better-flavoured ingredients do produce better food, but how much better?

Australia is blessed with high-quality, cheap table wine available for around $10 a bottle. What therefore happens if I make two dishes of beef bourguignon – one with the $10 a bottle wine, and one with a $50 bottle. Would you be able to tell the difference?

The finely tuned palates of Matt Preston or Stephen Downes might be able to, but the ordinary man in the street probably won't be able to tell the difference. The reason is that the wine is only one ingredient in a dish of many – beef, onion, garlic, stock, thyme, bay leaves, parsley, carrots, salt, pepper, mushrooms and bacon – so even though the wine is a prime flavour ingredient, the subtleties are lost in the mix. Finally you also have to factor in the skill of the chef. A skilful chef knows exactly how to blend these flavours and ingredients to bring about a great dish: how to brown the beef for flavour; how to reduce the sauce; how to taste and adjust the flavours. A good chef can make even an ordinary wine taste great in the final dish – but ninety-nine people out of a hundred would never be able to pick which wine was used.

Stock is flavoured water. Naturally, stock is so much better than water in cooking. It's easy to make and without it, chefs cannot cook many items. All soups and most sauces need stock. Stocks are not just made with the flavour from the bones, but also contain flavour from the mirepoix, bay leaves and herbs. Poach fish in it, poach beef in it; use it, love it, care for it. Good stock; good chef.

You cannot substitute stock you have made yourself with any commercially purchased product. Stock powders, cubes and liquid stocks in the end are salt, MSG and some flavour enhancers. They just don't cut it.

As an interesting note, I spent some time watching Chinese chefs and I noticed an interesting thing that Chinese chefs do with their vegetables that western chefs don't: they use stock to coat the vegetables. Take choy sum, for example. When I go to a Chinese restaurant and order a plate of choy sum, the chef blanches it in a weak chicken stock. He then heats a wok with a little oil, browns some garlic and onion, then adds the vegetable, some chicken stock, tosses it around a bit and thickens slightly with potato flour. The vegetable is coated with chicken stock. Taste this from a good Chinese chef and you will notice the difference between that and the standard, western way of blanching and then tossing in butter.

Chefs love butter, and who doesn't? We use less butter in modern cooking than we used to in traditional French cookery. We want our food to be lighter and healthier, particularly in an Australian climate that doesn't have the harsh European winters, so we now use much more olive oil and much less butter. However, butter remains an essential ingredient and one of the truly great flavours. Buy some high-quality, unsalted butter to get the pure, true flavour. Taste it. You can almost eat it in chunks like cheese, it's that good. When I worked at Lazars, we would only use unsalted King Island butter. It made a real difference. Such a great ingredient can make cooking a real pleasure.

I have a love–hate relationship with butter. It's the one food that I really crave, but with high cholesterol, I do avoid it because, like any addict, I can't just stop at just a little. Butter is at its greatest on toast; slabs of cold butter the size of railway sleepers, straight from the fridge so it melts just a little but still stays solid.

Fat is the natural ingredient used to sauté food. You need fat to fry onions or coat pasta or vegetables. All chefs have a small bowl of cold cubes of unsalted butter at their disposal during service. (The bowl usually also has some ice cubes to stop the butter from melting in the hot kitchen.) It is also used as a last-minute ingredient to finish many dishes and sauces, as in monté au beurre (which means to finish with butter).

A couple of cubes of whole butter added to a dish the minute before it is served will add a gloss and richness to the dish. Dishes such as coq au vin, beef bourguignon, osso buco, lamb shanks, curries, most braised and stew dishes all benefit from a final addition of monté au beurre. Just add the butter, stir though to melt and serve immediately. A saucier also uses monté au beurre to finish most jus and demi-glace sauces. It gives a sauce that final silky sheen and kick the chef is looking for.

One of the other great uses for butter is 'beurre noisette', or hazelnut butter, particularly used for fish, but can also used on pan-fried steaks and veal. It's simple to make. Just pan-fry a portion of fish in a pan (you might use half oil and half butter to do this). Remove the fish and any excess fat, add cubes of whole butter, swish it around so it melts and then turns to a hazelnut colour, and spoon over the fish. If you go too far, it will turn black and burn, but do it right and the flavour is fantastic.

The saucier is the highest-ranking chef in the kitchen and with good reason. To get promoted to the sauce section in a large kitchen is a mark of the confidence and respect that the chef has in you. It marks your achievement so far and indicates that you can indeed mix it with the best of your peers. To make sauces, you really need to understand cooking and the delicate balance between flavours. Essential to the art of great sauces is, of course, great ingredients, but it is so much more about cooking methods and the skill of the chef.

To concentrate flavours, chefs reduce sauces. In order to make good food and good sauces, you must understand this process. When we have a sauce in a pan and bring it to the boil, steam is produced. This means the water in the sauce is boiling. In order to increase and concentrate the flavour, we 'reduce' the sauce by boiling off the water, leaving a stronger flavour. Reducing a sauce also thickens it, so if you want a thicker sauce don't add flour, which will add a startchy taste, just reduce it.

This works really well in small quantities such as one or two portions in a pan, but does not work as well in large quantities (such as 10 or 20 litres). For this reason, good restaurants make sauces in bulk to a base sauce stage and then finish them to order for each meal. To make a sauce on order, add brunoise of onion, some mushrooms or peppercorns (or whatever your sauce is) to a pan and sauté. Next add wine, reduce, add base sauce, reduce, taste. Adjust. Add monté au beurre and serve. This type of sauce is usually made in the pan the meat or fish was cooked in. This means the juices and flavours that are released in the cooking process can be incorporated into the sauce. It puts into perspective the task a saucier has serving two hundred à la carte during a dinner service!

Gary Player, the famous South African golfer was quoted as saying, 'The more I practise, the luckier I get'. Meaning he was a great golfer because he worked hard at it. If you want to be a cook, you must practice, the more you cook the better you will be. There is no substitution for experience. It takes years to really learn how to cook – and it takes years before you can honestly call yourself a chef.

When I first started cooking, I would typically make a dish or item and then ask the chef to taste it. He would then season it with a little more pepper, some salt or lemon juice, maybe some butter – and he was always right. How did he know exactly what the item needed? How did he know exactly what quantities to add to finish the item to perfection? He just knew! Even cooking at home my wife or daughters will ask me to taste a soup and be in awe at how I can just say what to add and how much to add to improve and finish it. After a few years of cooking as an apprentice you start to get a feel for the taste and for the ingredients – you can just taste an item and instinctively know what to add or what to do.

Some people are naturally better than others and that's what makes a great chef. You can teach it, and it can be learnt, but it takes time; a long time.

Take Thai food, for example. I can cook Thai food: twenty years of cooking has taught me a lot; I have been to Thailand many times; eaten Thai food in family homes and in Thai restaurants where I am the only white guy there. I know what good Thai food tastes like (and not just the sanitised Thai food for foreigners in Phuket). But I know that I am like a good home cook compared to a real Thai chef. They can do the taste and add things like I could never do without several years working in a Thai kitchen. No matter how hard I try, I will never achieve this for Thai cookery.

Herbs are used by chefs to complement and enhance a dish. We all know that rosemary goes well with lamb and that parsley goes well with fish. But knowing and understanding each herb greatly expands the capabilities of a chef. Knowing which herb goes with what ingredient, when to add and how much to add. Herbs such as sage are used extensively in Italian food and thyme is used in French food, but what do they taste like? What will it do for the dish?

When I was young, dried herbs were purchased in small bags labelled 'mixed herbs' from the supermarket. We never used fresh parsley, basil, thyme, sage or rosemary. Why? I don't know, maybe because flavour really wasn't that important and they weren't available commercially anyway.

So we all know fat tastes good and is extremely satisfying, but the king of fat is duck fat. A secret ingredient that when used in cooking will turbo charge a dish, so much so that we even have a full method of cookery devoted to cooking in duck and goose fat: confit. This means to fully submerge an ingredient in duck or goose fat and slowly cook it. It's good, very good.

When ducks are roasted, they release a lot of fat. A good chef would never waste duck fat: chefs will collect it and use it in all sorts of things from sautéed potatoes to browning mirepoix. It's one of those special ingredients that you wouldn't usually have at home, but makes a restaurant meal something special.

I know what really good food is. I even know the science behind why I like fish and chips but the fact remains that I, like everybody else, still fight the craving for fat, salt and sugar. As a young chef, I would burn so many calories that no matter how much food I ate, or how much beer or wine I drank, I would never put on weight. Once I turned forty, all that changed. Now if I look at a burger or have a binge weekend, I put on weight. I find it hard to have just one glass of wine or one portion of dinner. A good meal is crying out to be eaten, a bottle of wine is crying out to be finished: 'Eat me, drink me! Eat me, drink me!' they scream. However, I don't want to become a slave to the plate or bottle like I was once a slave to the kitchen. So for now, I watch what I eat and even have some alcohol free days. That being said, at seventy-five, I plan to reevaluate the whole situation.

Statistically, with the exit close by, I should be able to indulge more without doing any serious harm.

Chapter 14

A big fat pig and a dead duck

Of all the foods we eat, of all animals that are slower and dumber than us, there are none that I hold in higher esteem than the pig and the duck. The pig in all its forms is truly an animal worthy of praise and thanks. Despite its unwillingness to sacrifice its life for our nourishment and enjoyment, being so tasty and versatile, the pig was always going to end up on a plate. Fortunately for the pig, a few thousand years ago and due to its unclean habits it did convince the Muslims and Jews that eating pork was dangerous to your health and soul; there was however no such convincing of Christians, Buddhists or any other religions.

The pig gives us roast pork with crackling on Christmas day; pork and chive dumplings at yum cha; bacon for breakfast in the morning; pork sausages to go with our mashed potatoes; ham hocks to make pea and ham soup; kassler to go with our sauerkraut; and ham and salami for our sandwiches to name just a few treasures.

A good friend has a great theory that there is no such thing as a great meal: it is more a combination of the occasion, who you are with, where you are, the smell and the ambience that all come together to make it a highlight of our life. When asked what his favorite ever meal was, my late father in-law always said sausages and onions while camping and fishing with his brother. It does tend to illustrate that my friend may be right.

It may be that some of my best life experiences with food involve the pig and the duck.

Roast pork, bacon and black pudding all bring back many happy childhood memories with my father. My first experience is, of course, the Christmas feast each year. As a child, it was a full, exciting day of waking up early, trying to stay quiet so as not to wake my parents – and peeking at the presents from Father Christmas. Relatives would arrive, drink and laugh, while I played cowboys and Indians with my brother. Then lunch was roast pork with crackling. We almost never had roast pork normally; it was too expensive. That one, small piece of crackling, one crisp, salty piece of loveliness was only ever possible on Christmas day. I would hover around my father carving the pork trying to steal an extra piece or one of those crunchy bits from the outside of the pork.

Bacon was also a treat. It was expensive so kids didn't get to eat bacon very often. It was more for Dad, but occasionally on the weekend he would make a cooked breakfast and fry eggs, bacon and black pudding. If we were lucky, and lurked around the kitchen long enough, we also got some.

Joanne and I were married in 1985. We were both twenty-one. We went to Adelaide and the Barossa Valley for our honeymoon. Sitting in a restaurant in Hahndorf, the German couple that ran the restaurant picked up on our shiny, new rings, our young love, and recognised us as the honeymooners we were. They fawned and fussed over us, gave us a complimentary bottle of German wine and told us to eat, drink and enjoy. I ordered the German mixed grill. The old German looked at me with a serious face and said, 'If you order the grill you have to eat it all, you know.' I took that as both a warning and a challenge.

The plate arrived and it was big: enough to survive a harsh German winter big. There was kassler (smoked loin of pork), pork sausage, black pudding, herb dumplings, potato and sauerkraut. I started eating, knowing full well that the old man was watching. He came over to the table several times to pour wine and encourage me. The food was great but there was so much of it. My final forkful created not only a memorable moment – but a lifelong love of kassler and sauerkraut.

I don't remember the first time I ever had a Chinese steamed pork bun. It was probably the late eighties when I was working at the Hyatt. I remember eating yum cha with the Asian chefs. (You can't really have yum cha without steamed pork buns and pork dumplings, so that's when it must have been.)

The best yum cha I have ever had was on my first trip to China at the Victoria Hotel in Guangzhou. It seats about eight hundred people and is always full for lunch. There were ten courses for lunch, and ten courses for dinner every day. We had a meeting with the chef and toured the kitchen. Then we settled down for lunch. The Chinese love pork and use it in all sorts of ways, especially for yum cha: roast pork in rice noodle parcels, pork and chive dumplings, shiu mai, pork and mushroom dumplings, pork spring rolls, barbeque pork in pastry, pork ribs in black bean. There were lots of other items, but the pork was memorable.

The highlight of the meal was a plate of suckling pig (only a few weeks old, it had been fed entirely on milk) marinated in red vinegar, garlic, bean paste and Shaoxing (Chinese cooking) wine, then roasted to a crispy skin. I had never had such a dish in Australia and would not know where to get it, so to have it again, I have to go back to China. Whenever I am in China I always have suckling pig, I never miss it.

Recently, I was left at home with my twenty-three-year-old, newly acquired, honorary son. He was the friend of my eldest daughter and was staying with us while he recovered from a knee injury. He had never had the pleasure of char siew pork, never had Chinese roast duck, and never had steamed pork buns. Knowing that life is fickle and it would be a shame for him to die without ever having the pleasure of a little piggy cooked this way, I took him to the Chinese area of Richmond. We had dinner and talked, then went for a walk. I went into the restaurant where I usually buy steamed pork buns for lunch if I am passing through the area. I exited with four steamed pork buns, two each.

'What are these?' he asked.

'Char siew bao,' I replied.

He tasted the bun and I could see the waves of pleasure flow over his face. He called them 'clouds of loveliness'. Just to be able to show somebody this for the first time was truly a special experience: not to share it would be a sin.

For Christmas 2008, one of my business partners gave me Neil Perry's *Balance and harmony: Asian food* cookbook. I open the book and start searching for pork recipes. I find gold in a recipe for sweet black vinegar pork belly. Looking at the recipe, I see it is in fact quite easy, so I cook it for my family. The acid of the vinegar, the richness of the pork, the sweetness of the brown sugar and the complexity of the Shaoxing brings much praise for Perry, and even a little for me, at the dinner table.

All flushed like a kid with a new toy, I invite friends over for dinner and cook it for them. They are amazed and think I am a god in the kitchen. I do give credit to Perry, but they don't believe it and think I'm just being humble. Get the book and cook the pork; you shouldn't miss this dish.

Despite visiting Asia many, many times, Joanne and I had never been to Bali. Convinced to go to by Anthony Bourdain, in 2010 we went for a holiday. On arrival, I'm on a mission to eat the pork at Ibu Oka. I discover that it is in the inland town of Ubud, about three hours drive from Seminyak, where we are staying. So we hire a car and a driver for the day and set off.

We find the restaurant is a casual, Asian-style, open-air establishment. It really only sells just one dish: the pork special. Each morning, about four whole pigs are slaughtered and roasted over a pit of hot coals, basted in coconut water continuously. The result is succulent, tender, roast pork with crispy coconut crackling. Add some spiced greens, sambal and some blood sausage and you have a dish famous the world over. Served on a paper plate, you sit anywhere you can find a seat. It costs about $3. Is it worth the effort and the travel? Yes, definitely.

Another delight in Bali is Balinese pork. Cubes of pork belly are cooked with Indonesian spices and shrimp paste. It's hard to describe as the Indonesian flavours are like nothing else. It's worth the travel just to try it – but don't eat in Kuta, the tourist restaurants remove all that taste for the foreigners.

I never dreamt that pork could be prepared and served in all these different ways. To discover it can, is to live the dream.

Now let's turn our attention to my other favourite animal sacrifice, the duck. Growing up, we never, ever had duck, it just wasn't the kind of food we ate. Even if we'd had a taste for it, there would never have been the budget for it. So, despite two loving parents, a roof over my head, health and happiness, I do feel that the pre pre-duck period of my life when compared to the post-duck period of my life was missing something special. Yes, it was obviously missing duck.

(The fact that I can break up my life into pre-duck and post-duck rather than pre-sex and post-sex says something about how highly regarded I consider the duck! Would I prefer crispy skinned Yarra Valley duck drizzled with Illawarra plum and garlic sauce to sex? Don't be stupid, of course I would have the sex but if I finished quickly so I could eat the duck it would not be my fault.)

The first time I had duck was while I was working as an apprentice at the Tavern. As mentioned, it was usually duck aux cerises (duck with cherries) or duck à l'orange (duck with orange). We would roast the ducks and reserve the duck fat for the potatoes. The chef would fuss over the sauce like no other dish. The result was truly great: rich as rich can be and full of flavour. I still make these duck dishes exactly the same way I learnt almost thirty years ago: it just can't be improved upon.

As you know, I have a distaste for almost all things offal, with a notable exception for duck liver. As an apprentice, pâté maison was a standard on every menu. The suburban restaurants used chicken livers while the up-market city restaurants used duck livers. Working at Lazars in King Street, we always used duck livers as part of what was then called a hors d'oeuvres platter. It would now be called a tasting plate.

This was cooked in my section and I fondly remember making sure that every day I would cook an extra one for myself. Often on a parmesan and egg crouton, gently fried shallots and a port glaze or marinated in olive oil, thyme and garlic, very gently pan-fried and placed on an oven-baked crouton, it was topped with fresh black pepper and mixed chopped herbs. Having this food available when I was financially struggling with a mortgage and car repair bills at home made life just a little bit easier.

But the peak of culinary perfection in regard to livers, even if it is made from goose rather than duck liver, has to be pâté de foie gras. High in fat and very rich in flavour, the result is heaven on earth. Real foie gras was used very little in the early days of my career as it was too expensive for all but the top restaurants. But now it is quite common in many restaurants: part of a dish might be topped with a small amount of foie gras. Eat and enjoy.

In Paris for the first time a couple of years ago, Joanne and I stayed near the Eiffel Tower – as many tourists do. As a chef trained in French food, I had dreamt all my culinary life of being in Paris. Finally, I was there, but the whole area was full of tourists – and like tourist areas anywhere in the world, most of the food is terrible. Friends have assured me that if I get out of the Champs de Mars area, the food gets better, but that is for the next trip.

Anyway, disillusioned with the local restaurants, we went to the supermarket. French supermarkets are very good, and we were able to purchase a great array of cold meats, cheeses and duck pâté for very reasonable prices. Being winter, we had the picnic in our room, complete with a bottle of champagne (and interleaved with marital commitments); it was the best picnic ever. Every hour on the hour, the lights on the Eiffel Tower sparkled for about 10 minutes. We spent the nights just watching the lights together and whenever I have duck liver pâté, I think of that night.

As much as the French love duck and do such a wonderful job with the bird as an ingredient, it is the Chinese who really take the duck to the height of gastronomic fame. My favorite dish of all time, my death-row meal, so to say, is Peking duck.

Those that know me know that I have a vision of what happens when you die. I have thought about it a lot. I'm not sure why, but I have. When you die, assuming that you can gain entry to heaven, you will almost certainly end up in a queue to get in. While waiting in this queue, you will be served Cointreau on ice. Once you have gained admittance through the gates of heaven, the first meal that will be served is Peking duck. But don't take the risk and wait, I could be wrong and the Hare Krishnas could be right: so eat Peking duck now.

As an aside, in China, Peking duck is known by the more politically correct name, Beijing duck. As you would expect, Beijing is the home of Beijing duck. Most restaurants there serve the dish and some are entirely devoted to this one, famous dish. One chain of restaurants, Quanjude, is said to sell over two million ducks each year. (Quanjude recently opened a restaurant in Melbourne, but I haven't had the chance to dine there yet.)

Now, there are a couple of different versions of Peking duck. China is a very big place and the food varies significantly from province to province, as you would expect. Canton, or its modern name of Guangzhou, is found in the south, not too far from Hong Kong. Around the world, Cantonese food is the most famous style of Chinese food. Hong Kong and most Chinatown districts around the world are dominated by Cantonese-speaking people. The Cantonese take food very, very seriously and have taken Peking duck to a whole new level.

For the uninitiated, the experience of Peking duck starts as a carving trolley arrives beside your table. The trolley is laden with a whole Chinese roast duck, small thin pancakes, batons of spring onion about 4 centimetres long and a type of hoisin based sauce. The duck is carved and wrapped in a pancake with a piece of spring onion and some sauce. The whole ritual and display makes it very enticing.

In Beijing, they tend to carve the meat and skin of the duck together and wrap in the pancake with the spring onion and sauce. But in

Guangzhou, Hong Kong and most Australian restaurants, they bring out the duck and only carve the crispy skin for the pancake, leaving the meat on the bone. The duck is then taken back to the kitchen, carved and used to make a second course of san choy bow. The chopped duck is cooked into another dish and served with iceberg lettuce cups. You simply fill the lettuce with duck, wrap and eat. Some restaurants even serve a third course of soup made from the bones.

If you don't want all the fuss and ritual of Peking duck, you will find roast duck, char siew pork and crispy roast pork hanging in the window of most Chinese barbeque restaurants. Add to noodle soups, serve on rice or just enjoy on their own; you'll find they are cheap and outstanding.

I have had very many great times taking people who have never eaten Peking duck before to eat the famous dish. Just being able to share and tell people about it fills me with joy and is one of the great pleasures you can have.

The men in my family don't share their feelings much. We talk about football, politics and the kids but not about feelings, not about emotions. But in 2005, my father was dying of prostate cancer and, knowing he would not be with us much longer, I had a very personal issue to attend to: I wanted to say thank you to him. I knew this was a unique opportunity. One I would regret if I missed, so I took him out to lunch. I didn't know how else to do it.

I took him to my favourite local Chinese restaurant for yum cha on a Sunday. We ate roast pork, Peking duck, pork and mushroom dumplings, scallops in black bean and lots more. I said, 'Thank you for being a good father,' and assured him I had had a great childhood. He didn't say much. Six months later he died and I was glad I had had the courage to do that lunch and speak with him.

Chapter 15

A chef's paradise

When the restaurant doors are closed or they get home from work, what do chefs eat? For me it was scrambled eggs; light, fluffy and slightly undercooked with sea salt and freshly ground black pepper. For other chefs I know it was Heinz baked beans on toast or soup and bread. Every chef has their own thing that they turn to when they don't want to cook.

It's naturally expected that a chef eats at work, which is true a lot of the time, but work is not really a place where you can relax and enjoy your food. Most of the time chefs eat leftovers. If you work the fish section, there might be one or two serves of cooked fish left over after all the tables have been served. A chef might throw it on a plate, add a little sauce, grab some vegetables from the entremetier and scoff it down while taking a 5-minute break before cleaning down their section. It's not really an ideal situation to enjoy your dinner.

Some restaurants have a staff meal. This can fall into one of two categories: the meal made by the chefs for the waiters and bar guys and the meal that the chefs cook for themselves. In general, chefs don't eat the meal they cook for the waiters. Designed to fill the stomach rather than delight the mind, it's just not up to our standard. A staff meal for chefs is usually a simple non-complicated meal such as a blanquette of veal, beef stew or pork-belly salad. If there is an Asian guy in the kitchen then he generally gets to cook the staff meal for the chefs. He usually cooks home-style meals from his country of origin. But to be able to sit down to a staff meal, you have to be one hundred per cent prepared and ready for service. If your mis en place is even slightly behind, you can forget about a staff meal. It's more important to have a good service than a good meal for yourself.

During the day a chef will graze. A bit here and a bit there, but contrary to popular opinion, most chefs don't eat a lot. But they know how to drink – at home and at work when they can get away with it. Cooking wine; cooking brandy; or even better, a cold beer in a hot kitchen. In the modern world of OH&S, drinking on the job is obviously not looked upon in a favourable manner and is even a sackable offence in big companies, but in the old days, even as an apprentice, I usually had a couple of glasses of wine at lunch and a scotch for dinner. When you are cooking all day it is work. Sure, it's nice eating restaurant standard food on a daily basis but you do lose some enjoyment when you eat standing at the bench or eating quickly before cleaning down your section.

To really enjoy food, you need to be able to take your time and relax. That's the difference between dining and eating. For the most part chefs eat, they don't dine. That's why half the time chefs don't eat at work. They will go anywhere else but work and eat anything else but what they cook at work, very often simple food like an omelette or some cheese and olives. Or, more commonly, Asian food. Be it the sharp fresh flavours of Thai fish sauce, lime and chilli or the sweet barbeque flavours of Cantonese cuisine, this is what I can sit down to relax and enjoy. Chilli is the most addictive ingredient of all. Once I started to eat chilli, things started to change. I started to change. Eating Asian food became my preferred meal. My taste in food was indicative of the change in Australian society over the same period. What was happening to me was a magnification of what was happening to Australia.

Chilli is a versatile product that can be used as an ingredient or a condiment but not one that comes naturally to those of us from European descent. First you start to use it as an ingredient, then you crave it as a condiment. As a condiment, it can be added to soy sauce as a dipping sauce or is obviously found in Chinese chilli sauce, sweet chilli sauce and dried chillies in oil. As an ingredient, it is used in almost everything Thai from the salads to the pad Thai noodles. Indeed, without chilli, there is no Thai food.

In no time at all I couldn't even eat a dim sim without chilli paste or sit down to a plate of char kway teow (already containing plenty of chilli) without asking the waiter for a side of fresh chilli or chilli paste. When I go back to flathead fillets with beurre noisette and capers, I find myself wishing for a side of chilli. I didn't plan it to happen, it just happened.

But it wasn't just happening to me – everybody else was picking up on it, too. Asian restaurants were becoming common, and not just Chinese restaurants but Vietnamese and Thai as well. Many start by eating Thai curries with their red and green combinations of chilli, lemongrass, garlic, fish sauce, lime leaves, red onion, galangal, coriander and shrimp paste. Finished with coconut cream and lime juice, they are such fresh, intense flavours that are nothing like any European dish at all.

Once you get used to the Thai curries you are ready for all things Thai. The salads are the most dramatic. A combination of any number of salad or meat ingredients topped with a dressing of fish sauce, lime, sugar and chilli. Once you start to eat Thai food there is no going back. You are addicted and life has changed.

There are different standards and grades of Thai food. There is what is called farang Thai, which is Thai food for foreigners. This is okay for beginners, but for those who us who become hard core, Thai Thai is much better. Thai Thai is what the Thai people eat. It is so packed full of flavour that it punches you in the face. Yes, it uses chilli, fresh, little, red ones that are hot, but the heat is balanced by the sweet, sour and salty flavours of the dish and ends up something that is like nothing a European chef could ever make. The chefs who do make these wonderful creations are sweet, humble, content, happy Buddhists put on earth to raise the overall average of the happy index for mankind.

So how do you find Thai Thai and how do you know the difference? Well, you should know it immediately. When you eat Thai Thai, it will be packed full of flavour rather than bland and soft. Sydney is blessed with many really good Thai Thai restaurants. Melbourne has a few, but most suburban Thai restaurants will be doing farang Thai.

If you are fortunate enough to go to Thailand, it is still not as easy as you would think. If you stay in a tourist area like Phuket, then the food is generally poor. Without flavour, it is made for tourists whom they assume are white people afraid of any real flavour (or, farang).

On my travels I have noticed that in all tourist areas from Bombay to Paris from Bangkok to Kathmandu there will be restaurants serving some local food as well as pasta dishes, hamburgers, club sandwiches, pizzas and spring rolls. They are serving what they think foreigners want but have neither the skill nor the understanding to do anything well. Avoid these multi-cuisine menus.

So be it Patpong in Bangkok, downtown Phuket, Darling Harbour in Sydney, Lygon Street in Melbourne, Champ de Mars in Paris or Connaught Place in New Delhi, the food will be generally poor and overpriced. You have to find where the locals eat to find nice food. If you are in Bangkok and you see a restaurant full of Thai and almost no white faces, then eat there. Especially if it looks a bit dodgy and the meal costs $2 there is a very, very good chance that you will get very, very good food. It might just be a noodle soup with duck but it will be great. Oh, and don't forget to add extra chilli.

Back in Australia, to eat good Asian food, go where the Asians are. In Melbourne, you'll find it in Victoria Street, Richmond or in Springvale. In Sydney, Sussex Street or Surry Hills; go to most Chinese restaurants in Dixon Street and you will eat ordinary food for Aussies, but take a closer look and see where the Asians eat and you will get better food. Chefs get to know where to eat, where to get that authentic taste, that real flavour and that's where we eat.

In Chinese restaurants where Asians eat, there is a whole secret menu that white people never see: the eel in black bean, the roast pigeon, the fish in XO sauce, the choy sum, the chive dumplings, the beans and pork mince in chilli oil and the salted fish fried rice. Go to China and you will be blown away by Chinese food. Even in the tourist areas, it's not too hard to find good Chinese food.

My point is that Asia and Asian food is heaven on earth both for myself and for most chefs. Indeed, many hotel chefs who travel the world somehow manage to end up in Asia, marry Asian women and never return. In every Asian city you will find the hotels full of these guys. They've changed; they are no longer Swiss, no longer Americans, no longer English and no longer Australians. Asia is a chef's paradise.

You even get to love the smell and the traffic. Follow the locals and take it easy. When you get back to Melbourne, you wonder if you really did the right thing coming back. Maybe you have should stayed and had duck soup and a tropical fruit platter every morning for breakfast at 10.30 am.

In the eighties when I started cooking, we were just starting to discover and enjoy Asian flavours and ingredients. In the last ten years, Indians have become the latest wave of migrants to Australia. Every migrant brings with them a small part of home in the food they eat and the way they do things. So the High Street Tavern restaurant where I did my apprenticeship in Ringwood is now the Punjabi Masala Indian Restaurant. Rogan josh has replaced porterhouse steak with beurre maître d'hôtel, aloo gobi has replaced rack of lamb with honey. Chicken tikka is now the national dish of England and take a look behind the kitchen door of any restaurant – not just the Indian restaurants – and you may very well find an Indian chef.

So what does this mean for hospitality? When most migrants arrive they set up cheap restaurants and takeaways based on the home cooking of their land of origin. We've seen this already with the enormous growth of Indian restaurants. They are almost always exactly the same, serving one style of Indian cooking: North Indian, Punjabi-style curries with Punjabi- and Delhi-style tandoori dishes. The curries are all served in little copper bowls with fake saffron rice and are preceded by samosas and onion bhajis. Tandoori chicken on a sizzle plate and naan bread to mop up the gravies.

In the north of India bordering on Pakistan is the Indian state of Punjab. The state is dominated by people of the Sikh religion with their sacred shrine, The Golden Temple, in Amritsar. The Sikhs are great travellers and migrants; they have come to dominate the Indian restaurant scene around the world. Sikh men often wear a turban and beard as they view hair to be sacred and not to be cut, ever. The name 'Singh' dominates the whole region and its people. Many Indians are vegetarians but the Sikhs are omnivores so have the marketing advantage of being able to serve tandoori chicken, rogan josh and goat curry, all made rich and satisfying for westerners by the liberal addition of ghee (butter fat) and cream.

India is a big place with over a billion people and as you would expect, the food varies from state to state, city to city and village to village. But in Australia, we eat almost exclusively Punjabi. Indian food has a reputation for being hot, chilli hot, but in reality, it's not that hot at all. The spices used are more aromatic like cumin, cinnamon, bay leaves, coriander seeds, and cardamom rather than loads of fresh chilli.

Chilli is used in south Indian food from cities like Chenni and Kerala. As you head further south towards Sri Lanka though, the food becomes more hot and spicy, using more coconut and chilli. They do away with plates and cutlery altogether, relying on banana leaves and your hands instead. Southern Indian food is virtually not served in Australia at all.

Another Indian state with great food is Gujarat. Indian migrants with the name, Patel, usually come from Gujarat. This is a very conservative area and was the home of Mahatma Ghandi. Like Ghandi, they have a vegetarian diet with no alcohol. The food there is eaten on a thali plate. A typical restaurant of the area does not have a menu as such, just whatever the chef has felt like cooking that day. You are given a large stainless steel platter with about four or five small stainless steel bowls. Twelve-year-old barefoot waiters arrive and fill the bowls with assorted curried vegetables, mini chapatis, baby samosas, onion salsas and sweet yogurts. They just keep coming back and refilling your bowls. Eat as much as you can but they will always be there to refill again. All this for a cost of about 100 rupees (about $2.50).

When I first started to travel to India, associates would take me out to hotels to eat dinner, but I used to press them to take me where they ate, not where they thought I wanted to eat. I discovered the Gujarati thali and never went back to a hotel. It was the $2.50 meal for me every time.

In Chenni they have fish coated in a coriander paste and cooked in banana leaves, crisp lentil pancakes, rolled and filled with spiced potato for breakfast. Add some sambar (a thin curry soup) and some coconut chutney and you have a common breakfast for 500 million people.

Everywhere you go in India there are Chinese restaurants, but they're not the Chinese restaurants you get in Hong Kong, Guangzhou or even Melbourne. They serve what is known as Chinese–Indian. The Indians are totally addicted to spice in all its forms, and simply can't eat even a piece of fruit without adding a masala of some sort. So when cooking Chinese food they add the Indian spices and you have a whole new cuisine.

Chinese–Indian restaurants are everywhere in India but Calcutta is truly home to this speciality. A small population of Chinese people who have been there for over a hundred years have formed a Chinatown district full of restaurants. The food there is twice as good as Chinese–Indian food elsewhere in India and trying to describe it is like trying to describe the colour blue to a blind man. There may be one or two small cafes selling this type of food to Indian migrants now living in Australia around the areas like Harris Park in Sydney, but in general, you can't get this food anywhere in Australia.

My reason for taking you on a selected short culinary tour of India is that from an Australian point of view, we have only just scratched the surface of Indian food. We still have a long way to progress in terms of the variety of Indian food we offer in our restaurants in Australia to come anywhere near the variety of really good food that is out there. India has the best vegetarian food in the world, and when travelling to India, it is the only time and place that I eat exclusively or predominantly vegetarian food and are more than satisfied in doing so.

In my career I have seen the advent of Asian and fusion food taking its rightful place at the table. It happened when young Australian chefs like myself started to work side by side with Asian chefs. Now young Australian chefs are working side by side with Indian chefs who are now making the staff meal – and it will change them, just like it changed me.

One day soon we will see more variety of Indian food on offer and it will start to penetrate the menus of international restaurants. Just as if you go to Jacques Reymond, you will notice that the menu has a Japanese influence, one day soon you will go to the latest hot shot chef's restaurant and it may well be fusion, Indian style. Don't be afraid or say it can't be done, young chefs will always seek the new and untried; they won't listen to the old bastard chefs and we will be glad that they didn't.

So Asia is a chef's paradise, start to travel and you will discover that there is a whole lot more out there than you ever thought possible. Don't be scared to eat, and don't forget the chilli.

Chapter 16

Bastardising food

Unfortunately, running a food business is a tough game and one of the hardest commodities to get in the food business is a chef. Chefs are in short supply. This has led to many businesses being structured in such a way that a less skilled cook can handle the work.

Look at desserts, for example. If you take the fine dining restaurants out of the equation, almost nobody makes desserts. Why? You try to find a good pâtissier willing to work for $35 000–40 000 in a pub or cafe. This person does not exist; a good pâtissier expects a lot more pay than that and they are few and far between. They can usually be found working in a patisserie or for a five-star hotel. Apart from them, nobody has a pastry chef on the books. Sure, chefs can cook desserts, but desserts are a very specialist area. You will usually find that stove cooks don't make dessert and dessert cooks don't work on the stove.

So where do all our desserts come from? From factories, that's where. Take a $2 mini pavlova, unwrap it and place on a 10-inch white plate. Decorate the plate with raspberry coulis (purchased in 1 litre squeeze bottles), add whipped cream, grated chocolate and fresh strawberries and you have a strawberry pavlova for $12.

Purchase a 12-inch lemon meringue pie, mark out ten portions, slice and place on a 12-inch rectangle plate. Add a scoop of pure cream this time, add some poached berries (purchased frozen) a sprig of mint and you have a dessert. Don't like lemon meringue pie? That's okay, the same supplier also has chocolate mud cake, flourless orange cake, black forest cake, sticky date pudding, carrot cake, baked ricotta cheesecake, pear and almond tart, the list goes on. Just order from the supplier, store in the cool room, slice, decorate and serve.

A different supplier will sell slightly different desserts all dressed up to look like they were made at the premises but in reality, they were made in a factory. Many of these products are in fact very good products, but my point is that the cook working in the cafe or pub most likely does not have the time, equipment or the skill to make these products anywhere near as good as the factory. So it becomes a matter of ease and economics to not make desserts.

What else can we buy? Meat? As a commis, my job was to cut, trim and portion the steaks. Most younger chefs (apart from those in fine dining) would never trim and portion steaks any more. They may not even know how. It's all purchased portioned and wrapped from big wholesale butchers. All you have to do is every couple of days count your stock, look at the bookings and place the orders. Most cooks no longer handle meat except to cook it.

Fish is the same. Once upon a time a restaurant would order whole fish that would be cleaned and portioned by a cook. Not any more. The seafood supplier or the fish wholesaler does all of this. Just order by the portion according to size, grade and weight. Delivered fresh to your back door already packed in foam boxes with ice shavings, just place in the coolroom until it gets ordered.

Vegetables can be ordered any way you like, all prepared in a factory and delivered to your kitchen by a refrigerated truck in the morning. Leave a message on the answering machine of your supplier after service and they will have it there for you by 10 am the next day. Potatoes no longer need to be peeled, they can be ordered in 10 kg bags peeled, sliced, diced, noisette, parisienne, chunks for roasting, whatever you like. They keep really well in the coolroom too, thanks to the added preservative. Want your carrots and onions peeled and delivered in 10 kg bags, too? No problem. Short on time and want the onions sliced as well? That's okay, just ask. Pumpkin cut, cabbage sliced, beans cleaned; the supplier can do almost all of this mundane work.

You'd think that stocks, soups and sauces would have to be made by the cook in the kitchen, wouldn't you? Some venues never make stock at all, preferring to use 2 kg tins of stock powder. You can get any manner of soups, also in the same 2 kg tins. Many venues don't even make mayonnaise, tartare sauce, demi-glace, hollandaise, velouté, béarnaise and they may not even make salad dressing. They probably make béchamel from milk and napoli sauce from 3 kg tins of crushed tomatoes and garlic from 1 kg buckets of crushed garlic. We now have a distinctive class difference in the kitchen: non-chefs, cooks, chefs and rock stars.

I thank my lucky stars I was trained in French food rather than Italian or even worse than that to have the misfortune of being an Italian chef. To be an Italian chef (or even just Italian) and having to face cafe after cafe and restaurant after restaurant defacing your heritage and defaming your cuisine would surely be enough to drive a real Italian chef mad. It must break Guy Grossi's heart.

Italian food is the most bastardised cuisine in the world. Italian restaurants are everywhere yet hardly any of them are actually run by Italians. Even fewer are producing food anywhere close to being classified as Italian. The worst of all are the combination pizza and pasta joints with big signs saying, 'Italian Restaurant'. They produce second-rate pizzas and second-rate pastas in cream sauces. Also on the menu is caesar salad, veal scaloppini, steaks, garlic bread and garlic prawns. But their biggest crime of all is the risotto. It's a good food/cost dish with a high profit margin so risotto is a common dish on these menus and, indeed, on all cafe and pub type menus but often, the wet rice they offer has nothing in common with risotto at all.

In my time as a hired gun I used to work 6 pm to 10 pm every Friday at one of these joints. The food was mass-produced, using every shortcut I had ever seen and some new tricks that I had never thought of before. They would not really even bother to make the standard tomato sauce. Sure, they opened tins of crushed tomatoes and put it in a pot, added mass-produced crushed garlic from 1 kg tubs and dried mixed herbs then heated up but it could not be called sauce. It didn't really cook at all; just heated it up and it was done. This is the base sauce for many pasta dishes and tastes nothing like a tomato sauce made with real ingredients by a real Italian chef.

The risotto at this joint was a real crime. Made with long grain rice, (repeat long grain rice, no mistake, these cowboys didn't even bother to use arborio rice), they would just add some ingredients to cooked rice and finish with stock, cream and cheese. Wet rice for God's sake is an embarrassment to a chef, but it must be heartbreaking to an Italian chef.

The coolroom was a mess, the staff toilets stank of stale urine and the storeroom had food falling all over the floor. The kitchen cloths were bacteria infested salmonella farms so I brought in my own cloths each week. The team was young, the chef was twenty-two and the owner was twenty-seven. They were take no prisoner, hard-arse guys who really didn't care about much other than making money, fast cars and women. They had an abundant supply of all three. Who can blame them for this attitude when the restaurant was always full; with three hundred covers on a Friday night and three fifty on a Saturday night, money just rolled in. I got a hundred bucks for my four hours and even then took the money with shame. I didn't put that one on my resume. It destroys my soul to have the skill, experience and ability to cook good food but to pump out empty lifeless calories on a plate. However, it's all well and good to be proud, but it doesn't pay the bills.

So why do customers turn up day after day and eat this rubbish paraded as Italian food? They just line the pockets of someone who knows nothing at all about the Italian culture, history or cuisine. Although he runs the business like an amateur production he makes so much money that I am left wondering where is the justice in the world. Why not just go to KFC? At least it has flavour.

Italian restaurants are also made into big franchise chains with outlets all over town. Again, it has little to do with the food. The Italians are a proud people with much to be proud of – they have given us mozzarella, gorgonzola, taleggio, pancetta, balsamic vinegar, salami, pizza, pasta, osso buco, Italian anchovies and much, much more. They are masters and fanatical about coffee, ice-cream and veal dishes. They use rosemary, garlic, sage and parsley with finesse and judgment that stems from 2500 years of cooking – and you can see it, smell it and taste it. All this and I have not even mentioned the wine which is vastly underrated and under sold in Australia, so much so that it is often completely forgotten about. But none of this is evident in these Italian franchises.

But your favourites may not be the savoury dishes. Like my wife, they might be the sweet dishes. I would be in heaven over a simple pasta with olive oil, fresh tomato, Italian anchovies and basil. Add a glass of pinot grigio and I'm satisfied, but Joanne will be eating small portions while waiting for the dessert. Mascarpone with baked peaches, strawberries in balsamic vinegar with pistachio ice-cream, espresso granita with baked amaretti plums, pumpkin panna cotta with candied walnuts, biscotti parfait with sambuca, strawberry or fig tart with clotted cream.

The Italians know how to make dessert. This is why some great traditional dishes – such as tiramisu, tartufo, gelato, zabaglione and baked ricotta cheesecake – have become mass-produced standard items. All great dishes that have become fodder for everybody but the Italians.

Take a walk down a tourist street and look at the plates on the tables of the restaurant diners. What do you see? Diners might start with the antipasto platter consisting of ingredients for which the cooks have played absolutely no part in making. Cheap plastic olives from a jar, grilled vegetables purchased in two kilo buckets, grilled artichoke hearts from a tin or 2 kg tub, Australian-made cheese, salami slices, dried tomatoes from the same tub and toast made from bread not crafted by the chef but superbly toasted. You get my drift.

Next to the antipasto platter will be frozen, crumbed calamari rings with two pieces of mesclun and ready-made tartare sauce, pizza that looks like it's from an American fast food chain, cream sauce pastas like a carbonara or funghi that are so heavy with fat that just a small amount satisfies the primitive brains of the uninitiated, pasta sitting in a lifeless heap collapsing on a plate screaming, 'Whatever happened to al dente?'

There are also huge, green-lipped frozen mussels from New Zealand that any self-respecting Italian would spit out if ever they got into their mouth, herb breads of tasteless bread and dried herbs, something called fritto misto which resembles cardboard pieces shaped into various seafood animals then crumbed or battered and deep fried. Then the finale is the powdered soap they put on every table and claim to be Parmesan cheese. I don't think so.

These so-called restaurants are designed around two concepts: low food cost and monkey see monkey do versions of common well-known Italian dishes. But these dishes are not the original simple working man's food of Italy. They are the bastardised versions that are on sale in every tourist area in every city in every country in the world.

After that walk down the street we are left asking a serious question. Who is the stupid one? Me, or the diners who frequent these dining establishments? Day after day, week after week and year after year they fill the coffers of these restaurateurs with money, and lots of it, for most of these are very successful restaurants serving hundreds of happy customers. Open a restaurant serving real Italian food and you will be much happier, have better karma and be much more satisfied, but I am fairly certain you will not be rich.

For the sweet lover and the coffee lover there is still a reason to go Italian: Brunetti. I will often drive the 50 kilometres to the inner city area from my home in the suburbs just to sit with Joanne for an afternoon of coffee and cake at Brunetti in Carlton. Round trip, that's 100 kilometres. When you get there, you will see that there must be a lot of other people burning vast amounts of fossil fuels producing copious amounts of greenhouse gases just for a coffee and a cake at Brunetti too.

The place is huge: it must be the biggest and best coffee and cake shop in Australia and it's full. Grab an empty seat if one becomes available. The range and quality of the cakes, biscuits, chocolates, nougats and pastries available are too much to mention here. Add nice sandwiches and rolls and a gelato bar and there is something for everyone.

Recently taking my seventeen-year-old daughter out for driving practice, I had her drive to Carlton for a coffee at Brunetti. She was blown away that such a place could exist and that it was there any time for her. A great discovery for a seventeen year old.

Many of the television celebrity chefs go to Italy, often the Tuscan region, to do their TV shows and write their cookbooks. Most of these cooking shows and TV chefs do a great job of showing the food of Italy. If you really do like Italian food like I do, then do some research and find the real Italian restaurants in your city that are run by Italians. They won't have a menu with the usual pizza and pasta dishes on them, they will have a much more creative menu, but one based on the simple cooking of basic Italian ingredients. They may be hard to find in the outer suburbs, so you will probably need to travel to the more avant-garde inner city areas.

If you like to cook good Italian food at home then find a good Italian deli in your area and get a good Italian cookbook. Not one made by a popular women's magazine or TV show, but one by a real chef who can really cook.

As an Australian, I wish I had the rich cultural heritage of food and wine that the Italians have. To have grown up making our own wine and olives, eating real cheese and drizzling olive oil on some homemade pasta. It must feel great to have all this in your DNA, but I'm not so sure I could cope with the heartache of what is paraded as Italian food defacing your DNA. Being of Scottish descent, I am safe from this – nobody has ever really tried to popularise haggis.

I know almost nothing about Mexican food because when I was cooking there were almost no Mexican restaurants around. In much the same way as Italian food has been cheapened and mass-produced, Mexican food has also been popularised by the big-money, franchise operations in the form of Tex Mex. From my knowledge of the culinary world I am pretty sure that what they produce has little to do with Mexican food. Once again the simple food of a noble culture has been put through a corporate machine. Cheap shredded cheese and canned jalapenos served on plates and paraded as Mexican food. How many professional chefs are working in Tex Mex kitchens? Good question.

In my hired gun times I was once sent to a Tex Mex restaurant. I discovered that in a normal European kitchen the microwave is used to melt butter, but in the so-called Mexican kitchen, the microwave is king. Everything is prepared, spooned onto a plate, coated with cheese and microwaved. After said microwave cooking, it is then topped with avocado dip, sour cream and tomato. Avocado dip from a tub, tomato from a tin, refried beans from a tin, pre-sliced jalapeno peppers from a jar, spices from a 600 gram jar of Mexican spice, tacos and tortillas from packets. Open, open, zap, zap. Now you're a chef.

But Mexican food does have all the elements of what I am sure is really good food. A combination of poor people, Spanish heritage and good ingredients is bound to be a recipe for good food. Where do you get it, though? I don't know. To really understand Mexican food I suspect you would need to go to Mexico and find where the taxi drivers stop for lunch or follow a family home from church on a Sunday and gate-crash their family meal. But you probably won't find it in the four-star hotel that you're booked into or that famous street of restaurants in the tourist district. Ask your concierge where they eat, not where they would send you to eat.

A few serious chefs have travelled to Mexico and followed a family home or eaten with taxi drivers to gain the real understanding. Hopefully they can spread their knowledge to young Australian chefs and the public. This gives us something to look forward to because from the passion of one or two chefs, good food and good recipes spread and we will be treated to some foods we have never tasted before. Just as we have only scratched the surface of Indian food, one day we will get to understand Mexican food for that is the way of the culinary world: good food can only hide away for so long.

I sit in a cafe drinking cold beer. I'm in Manila, Philippines and I have a serious question on my mind. What's for dinner? It's 3 pm and my work is done. Three days into a four-day trip I have spent the morning giving a pep talk to one hundred trainee cooks at a local culinary school. I ask them a question that's been on my mind for some time. 'What happened to Filipino cuisine?' I get one hundred blank looks back. They're not really sure what I mean, but let me explain.

This is my third trip to Manila. It's always exciting to go to a new country and experience their culture, tradition and food. On my previous two visits I had asked local associates to take me to a typical Filipino restaurant. Both times I had been taken to the same restaurant, completely independently. Each time I had enjoyed the food, a style that is hard to describe. It's a bit Spanish, a bit Chinese and bit western. Crispy fried pork knuckle, sautéed greens with fish sauce and adobo. I asked myself, 'Is this the only Filipino restaurant in town?'

Tonight, however, I have no associates to take care of me. Normally, in these circumstances, I take a walk and eat some local food but alas there is no local food on offer. Local food has been discarded for fried chicken, steak sandwiches, nachos and burgers.

There is a whole strip of about fifteen restaurants close to my hotel. The area is near a shopping centre and cinema, it's not a food court but a fully-fledged restaurant dining strip with indoor and outdoor dining areas. None are Filipino. There are two additional restaurants that do actually have a couple of Filipino dishes on the menu: Las Paella and Freska Seafood. But these are by no means Filipino restaurants: even their menus are dominated by burgers, spring rolls, pasta and pizza. They don't inspire much confidence.

All these restaurants look to have been created from the same concept regardless of the style of food. It's like they all owe their gestation to the same marketing programs that gave us every other franchise food chain in the world. All have smiling young staff with polo shirts sporting the company logo and a standard procedure for everything from offering a drink to the up-selling of side orders. All straight from the, 'Would you like fries with that?' fast-food university.

There is a strong likelihood I will end up having a burger or steak sandwich for dinner. I see the American fast-food takeover everywhere I go but here in Manila, it is most stark. Driving around the city I see an explosion of KFC, McDonalds, Starbucks and even Kenny Rogers Roasters. Add to this a whole industry of local copycat businesses: it's a real, soulless, fast-food nation that surrounds me.

Fried and roast chicken are the scourge of cities all over the world. No matter where I go I see the same soulless food purchased, served and eaten by locals, bypassing their own indigenous cuisine for the exotic

American food. Even in countries where KFC or Kenny Rogers have not penetrated, you get an abundance of local copies. In Dhakka, Bangladesh, you won't need to go far to get California Fried Chicken or Hollywood Chicken. In Jedda, Saudi Arabia, I see the same fried chicken on every second corner. They're everywhere in China but have not taken over yet; you can still get good Chinese food anywhere. Why people would prefer to eat generic brand fried chicken when they can have great local food for half the price I don't really understand. Okay, I do understand that they may see it as sophisticated and exotic and soon get hooked on the fat, salt and sugar.

The bottom line is that these outlets are there for a reason. They must be doing business. Fried chicken must be popular; why else would there be so many outlets? But by any measure, it is bastardisation of food and bastardisation of culture and it hurts me to watch.

I don't want the world to become one, I don't want to kill individual culture. But I am not innocent, even I have blood on my hands. When I see the Starbucks sign, be it in Beijing, Manila, Singapore or Hong Kong I think, 'Fantastic, good coffee.' I've had a Big Mac in Beijing after a week of Chinese food and I've had a Chicken Maharajah burger in India. But tonight, as I eat a steak sandwich and drink a Carlsberg beer, I do so with sadness.

Chapter 17

One, big, fusion pot

From a chef's point of view, when I look at well-known dishes, I can see that most dishes come from one of two origins: there are those that come from poor people and those that were made for rich people. There doesn't seem much food in between. (You must bear in mind, of course, that I am a chef and not an anthropologist, so these are my observations from standing at the stove cooking, not from studying at university.)

The French kitchen is full of dishes that were basically made by chefs cooking for the elite. These types of dishes generally incorporated expensive ingredients, the richness of dairy products such as butter and cream together with more exotic meats and more complex cooking methods. (Lobster thermidor, chateaubriand, sauce béarnaise and tournedos Rossini come to mind.) Over time, these inventions also became famous in the area and part of the national cuisine.

A number of factors contribute to the development of a national or even regional cuisine. It seems to me that throughout history, poor people have been very good at creating great food with a particular style and local ingredients that over time became national dishes, or at least a famous regional dish. A few cases in point.

There are many stories about the origin of the famous fish stew from the Provençal town of Marseille, bouillabaisse. As you will find with many classical dishes, it is generally thought to have originated from fisherman cooking the cheap leftovers into a stew and from there, the basic recipe would have been taken by chefs in the area and refined to the more luxurious dish we see today. A basic poor man's dish has been enhanced for restaurant patrons. But this took place over hundreds of years in an era when transport was slow and difficult compared to today. In those days, all food was, by definition, regional.

A cheap peasant dish, Irish stew is made with the cheapest and most available ingredients by poor people who had little else to eat – lamb or mutton, potatoes, carrots, parsley and onions.

Another basic stew, beef bourguignon from Burgundy in France, is made from ingredients common to the area – red wine, garlic, onions, mushrooms and herbs. This is another example of a poor man's food refined by chefs with the addition of bacon and sophisticated cooking methods.

Almost every part of the world has its own soup or simple broth made from whatever ingredients are available in the local area such as minestrone from Italy, cock-a-leekie from Scotland, borscht from Russia, French onion soup from France, goulash from Hungary and miso soup from Japan.

Another way that a national or regional cuisine is created is to use the available local ingredients that an area has in abundance – this could be cheese, spinach, mustard, wine, cabbage, potato, seafood, in fact, anything. Often a region develops a history of local produce that over time becomes a trademark of that region. French food, Spanish food, Thai food, Indian food, English food, even Russian food has its own style. It's only natural that the old world has its own style of food: they have had thousands of years to develop products, ingredients and dishes.

Due to fast, efficient, modern and international transport, the development of local cuisines that rely on local ingredients is now effectively dead for all but a few fanatical chefs and new generation hippies wanting to save the world by serving food with low 'food miles'. Strawberries out of season? No problem, fly them in from California, and bring some cherries while you're at it. Want to put English stilton on your cheese platter? That's okay, just pick some up from that specialist cheese shop up the road.

Our pantries are full of ingredients such as Dijon mustard from France, balsamic vinegar from Italy, Shaoxing wine from China, wasabi from Japan, chilli sauce from Thailand, spices from India and pickled herring from Holland. All these ingredients are used by creative chefs and good home cooks on a daily basis. There is no need to create a localised food speciality so the whole world becomes one, big, fusion pot.

Preserving food was originally a necessity in order make it available over the long, harsh European winter. Cheese is one product that springs to mind. France is a country of three hundred cheeses while India, where the cow is sacred and dairy products form an essential part of the diet, has only one cheese. Why? Because of the more temperate climate, milk is available all year round, and there is no need to preserve it. But in Europe, the need to preserve the milk over winter means that every village or town in Europe would have made its own cheese. Over time, the methods of cheese-making vary and you end up with hundreds of different cheeses distinctive to each region. This then naturally becomes a distinctive part of the local diet – as do other preserved foods which include hams, sauerkraut, pickles, dried beans, wine, spices and salami – and a regional cuisine is born.

Ever since I was an apprentice at Box Hill TAFE in 1982 the question has always been, 'What is Australian food?'

Australia's indigenous peoples have a long history of hunting and gathering native animals and plants, and following the land and the seasons both in the bountiful and lean times. Both cooking and preparation methods were varied and specialised, as were region-specific delicacies such as shellfish or particular bush foods. They used ingredients such as fish, shellfish and native animals with native seeds and berries to flavour their food.

There have been a number of very good restaurants utilising these bush food ingredients and there was a time when it was thought that bush foods – and ingredients such as lemon myrtle, wattle seeds, quandongs, wild limes, bush tomatoes, kangaroo and rosella flowers – might inspire a uniquely Australian cuisine.

But the lack of large commercial availability meant that these ingredients never made it into mainstream cooking and never captured the imagination of the vast bulk of Australian chefs and the public. The one exception to this is kangaroo which up until recently was considered dog food and not even legal for human consumption in most states. However, it has now has become that one quintessentially Australian ingredient that is on the menu not just in Australia but also in many other parts of the world.

From white settlement to the Second World War, there wasn't really much change in the type of food or styles of cooking in Australia. When Europeans first arrived, they were unsure of many of the varied plants and animals, and, on the whole, were more set up and comfortable emulating the way they ate back in England. This has persisted until recently when Australia opened up its borders and kitchens to new cultures and multiculturalism irrevocably changed our plates and our palates.

I was fortunate enough to have been born at just the right time to be changed by the food that we as Australians ate. While academics pondered the question of what it meant to be an Australian, meat loaf was being replaced with Thai green curry, apples were being replaced with mangoes and Irish stew was being replaced with aloo gobi from the Punjab. Multiculturalism had arrived and while we developed our own style of food – fusion food – that incorporated the food of our Asian migrants with our English heritage and French training it turned out that the rest of the world was doing it as well: it wasn't uniquely Australian after all.

So, has Australia developed its own unique cuisine? No, sadly, it hasn't. There simply hasn't been time and now with cheap airline travel, the world is a very small place. I doubt that we will ever develop a distinctive Australian cuisine. The world has moved too fast and already blended into one.

Chapter 18

Culinary solutions

So how does a chef like me make a living in 2012? Where am I at today? After I took a redundancy from Crown Casino in 1998, the bull was working at a restaurant/nightclub/function venue that only opened for dinner on Friday and Saturday nights. The owners of the venue seemed to have a lot of money but no idea how to run a restaurant business. They survived for quite a while because of the long line of young people paying good money just to walk through the door and then get drunk on overpriced alcohol in the nightclub.

The bull had free rein. He could do anything he liked without too much pressure because they had no idea how to run the food side of things, anyway. He asked me to be his sous chef, offered me a very good salary and basically offered me an easygoing job with reasonable hours.

I knew that if I took this job, I would be cooking for the rest of my life. So I made a resolution that I would never take a permanent job cooking again. I told him I would work for him, but on casual rates only. I wanted to be able to come and go as I pleased. He accepted this, but still wanted me full-time.

I had other things in mind. I had teamed up with Stephen Tryon, another chef from Crown Casino. Stephen ran the culinary training section at Crown that involved training for over four hundred cooks and chefs. He was a great chef and had all the training skills. I had the small business knowledge. Together we made a good team and formed a new business: Culinary Solutions Australia. At first we trained people in food safety and HACCP (Hazard Analysis and Critical Control Point), an international system of food safety.

When Crown opened, food safety was taken very, very seriously. Every cook, every chef and every kitchen steward received training in basic food safety and HACCP, even if they had already been trained in this area before. It was important work: if Crown had a food poisoning incident it would be on the front page of every newspaper and lead every news bulletin. Crown was streets ahead of the rest of the industry in food safety standards and the Kennett government was introducing new food safety laws for the whole industry after a number of food poisonings in the Asian restaurants and food businesses.

Stephen and I were ready to train and assist the rest of the industry in implementing these new laws. It's tough to start a new business and the growth of Culinary Solutions Australia was slow at first. There were also plenty of other chefs jumping on the bandwagon at the same time, but over the years, we have learnt to adapt and change to survive.

In 2007, another chef joined us. The three of us are all Hyatt chefs, we had all worked in Plane Tree and all three of us were Crown chefs. We have now been going for thirteen years. The early years of the business were very tough though: we basically didn't draw any salary for about eighteen months. During this time I worked for the bull and for an agency as a hired gun.

We started as a food safety company but then moved on to become an assessment company, carrying out exams for chefs. Say, for example, a guy had been working as a cook for ten years but had no formal qualifications. We would watch him cook, interview him, look at his resume, get written work and references together to form enough evidence to issue him with his Certificate III cooking qualification. Another type of client might be a cook from overseas who had overseas qualifications, but not Australian qualifications. Again, we would compare their overseas qualifications, watch them cook, interview them and then issue them with an Australian qualification. We became very well known for this type of work.

Sometimes, life happens by accident. I would never have thought about doing this kind of work but all of a sudden, Stephen and I were specialists in this area and were being called upon to travel to all sorts of places to do this work. It's great because I get to be around kitchens, be around cooking and be around chefs without having to front up for work each day in a starched white jacket and prepare the mis en place. For the first time in my life I was not locked in that one small room all day, every day. I now travel, not just around Australia, but all over the world. As the business progressed, we were asked to travel to India, Nepal, Thailand, China, Sri Lanka, Bangladesh, London – almost anywhere, but mainly Asia. We have relationships with cooking schools in Kathmandu, Manila and Vietnam; the world is much smaller than it was when I started cooking in 1982.

All that travel changes you in just the same way that food changes you. When you change the food you eat, you become a different person. Visit a dozen temples in various parts of India and you start to understand the philosophy of the people. I learnt contentment from sitting with them and eating the most basic meal of dhal, rice and roti. And I started to wonder about my life characterised by ambition, restlessness and competition with others. For the first time, it was not about gaining more, being a better chef, cooking better food, making more money. My life became more about enjoying the ride.

In 2005, we had a contract to train and conduct exams for Thai cooks in Bangkok. The project lasted a couple of years and we partnered with my Thai architect/restaurateur mate, Ped. The project was to gap-train good Thai chefs and accredit them so they could come and work in Australia. There was, and still is, a large demand for good authentic Thai chefs in Australia.

I spent a lot of time with Ped and a lot of time in Bangkok, always visiting the local Buddhist monastery where the chief monk was a teacher and mentor for Ped. We would arrive about 11 am with offerings of food: duck red curry, rice with salted fish, green vegetables in fish sauce and chilli, papaya salad, prawn and peanut salad, vegetable green curry, pineapple fried rice and an abundance of tropical fruit. By tradition, the monks cannot eat after 12 pm so between 11 am and 12 pm, about eight monks would all sit around a low round table and eat lunch of different offerings from the various locals, including us.

We would sit on the floor around the monks and chat while they ate. The chief monk was always very interested in our project and my travels. After the monks had finished eating, we would eat the leftovers. The food was always really good. Simple, fresh, Thai flavours: salty, sour, sweet and chilli.

After lunch, we would have a private audience with the monk who would advise and encourage us. This seemed like a pretty good system to me. After witnessing the calm, tranquility and contentment of the Buddhist lifestyle, I embarked on a study program to find out more. (The Dalai Lama is often the first port of call for would-be western Buddhists as he has co-authored many books that are readily available such as *The Leader's Way*, *The Art of Happiness* and *Becoming Enlightened*.)

Long hours waiting in airports and sitting on airplanes was giving me a lot of time to contemplate my future. The choice was, in fact, quite easy, but the step was big. After a lifetime of ignoring the spiritual side of life, I made a decision to be a Buddhist. To me, Buddhism offered a way to get off the relentless cycle of restlessness and ambition that is the life of a chef; a way to live my life aligned with the goal of happiness. I didn't even have to believe in God or attend temple and I could eat pork, duck or whatever I liked. (Alcohol is discouraged, but not forbidden.)

When working as a chef your life is broken up into neat 30-second parcels, the chef calls table five and you have 2 minutes to plate up the food. Not two and a half minutes: 2 minutes. Life as a Buddhist provides the balance that I never had. Ambition is now less relevant and life is more relaxed.

I am glad that earlier in my career I didn't try to become a rock star chef. I probably would have become a very one-dimensional person. My marriage may not have survived and I wouldn't have seen my children grow up. That 20-minute break, that day when I had had enough, when I had no mis en place left and was staring at another two hundred for dinner, decisions were made that set in motion of a huge chain of events. Just one day can be very important.

In the years following my exit from the kitchen chefs have changed, they have been forced to clean up their act. Much of the aggression of my day is no longer tolerated by Generation Y, human resource managers and society in general. Chefs have had to learn to get along with people because they are no longer locked in the back room. The preferred role model for a twenty-first century chef is now much closer to Eric Ripert rather than Niccolo the old bastard chef and that's probably a good thing.

My work now is varied and interesting. I am finally on the other side of that big door, eating in the restaurant instead of cooking in the kitchen. I have got to know different cuisines and styles of food that I would never have been able to see and taste in Australia. The way food changes as you travel around different parts of India; the difference between a Bangladeshi curry, a Punjabi curry and even a Sri Lankan curry. I get to enjoy an Indonesian charcoal-grilled fish with sambal in Bali or a hotpot on a cold, snow-covered winter's day at the foot of the Great Wall near Beijing.

Over the years, there have been other chefs who have tried to copy our business model, but have failed. We survive because we have created a critical mass of clients, diversified our business and made a name for ourselves. To do this is very hard. Just to find enough clients to get paid on a regular basis is extremely difficult and I would not want to start all over again. We had to diversify and do all sorts of things from selling training books, kitchen consultancy and recipe management software to training and working in TAFEs to survive. Finally, in 2012, after fourteen years, I am confident that I don't have to go back to the pans again.

So, after almost thirty years in and around the trade of restaurants and being around chefs, was it all worth it? For me it was and still is. I first and foremost identify myself as a chef. I still consider myself a chef, even though I spend more time at a computer than I do at the stove. It has been the single biggest defining factor in my life other than marrying my wife, Joanne.

I love the fact that I know what really good food is. To be able to sit down and know what to order from a restaurant menu is great. Last year I was in Hong Kong with Joanne and our two daughters on a family holiday. By coincidence, some close friends were also there at the same time. I was given the task to find us a restaurant for dinner. I booked a private room for eleven people down by the Star Ferry terminal on the Kowloon side. The others were not interested in the menu, leaving the ordering to me.

Instead of ordering from the Aussie–Chinese menu, I ordered the eel in black bean sauce, roast goose, chive dumplings, scallops in XO sauce, Chinese spinach, choy sum, steamed chicken with ginger and eel with honey. Lots of dishes my friends would not normally order. They loved them and just being able to share good food with good friends like this is one of the perks of being a chef. Being able to introduce people to food they have never had before is exciting.

About 20 kilometres from my home is a big shopping centre with two cheese shops. Each has a temperature-controlled room with ripe cheeses from all over the world: cheese that is actually ready to eat and at its optimum right now. If I have people over for dinner at our place, I make the trip and buy some ripe brie, stilton or taleggio. The joy it brings them is worth the travel; many people have never eaten ripe cheese before. Cooking duck à l'orange for dinner guests or making some ice-cream is great. I get a real kick out of it. There was a time when I was still working as a cook and I lost the passion for cooking. But now I love it more than ever. I love that I can do it – and I love that I don't have to do it every day.

I forget that not everybody knows food like I do. I can sometimes take it for granted that everybody has eaten a piece of cave-ripened taleggio, but not everybody has eaten Peking duck, not everybody has eaten foie gras, and not everybody knows how to cook pork belly. But I have all this and much more. I feel very privileged because I am a chef.

Being able to work and survive as a professional chef in good restaurants and bad pubs, in good hotels and old people's homes has given me the confidence to do anything I put my mind to. If I can handle life as a chef then I can do anything that life throws at me. Being a chef teaches you a sense of urgency and a sense of doing it the right way. A chef does not waste time; there is no time to waste. A chef is always well prepared because you know that if you are not, then you will be devoured when the moment arrives, sucked into a whirlpool of failure and ridicule. When you fail as a chef you fail big time – and everyone knows it.

All over the world, people love food. Being a chef means I instantly have something in common with whoever I meet under any circumstances. When traveling, people want to show me their culture, heritage and food. They seek your approval and are more than generous as hosts. I have learnt to be generous and humble. Even the great rock star chefs don't know it all and can still learn from a street vendor in Bangkok or Delhi.

After almost thirty years in the business, I know I still have a lot more to learn. I know almost nothing about Spanish food, Mexican, Arabic, African or South American food. The world is my oyster and I intend to suck on it as hard as I can for as long as I can.

I've been to the Royal Mail in Dunkeld for the ten-course degustation menu. Ten courses with matching wines in a style and a standard of food I have never seen before. Now I have booked the fourteen courses at Ku Da Ta in the new Singapore Marina. I know it's more entertainment than food but, well, I like this sort of entertainment. At least I do when I am in the dining room and not the kitchen. Like a kid before Christmas, I know how many days to go.

Being a chef means that I can appreciate food like this on a whole different level to people who are not a chef. I'm no better than a truck driver or a school teacher, but I know my area of expertise and I know food.

I recently went to Vietnam for the first time. It was a culinary feast every day, from eating noodle soups on the street and dining where the locals eat to eating in fine-dining restaurants. Travel is one big culinary tour and I am in the box seat. I never thought I would be, but that is where life and cooking have taken me.

My work takes me to different restaurants every week. I get to see chefs cook and I enjoy their company. Like a retired sportsman who becomes a coach, I have found a way to stay involved with what I love but do it at a level that my body and wife can tolerate.

For me, the journey is far from over and my life so far as a chef has been very rewarding. I am not a rockstar chef, but neither do I need to be. My life now is happier and more contented than it has ever been. Being a chef has given me much more than it has ever taken. But I have only ever been able to do it with the love and understanding of my wife, Joanne. I still drink too much and now eat more food than my forty-nine-year-old body can metabolise, but I have managed not to become a drunk, managed not to become a fat man, managed to stay married and managed not to become an old bastard.

To this day, I am still the black sheep of the family – a Buddhist with a craving for Peking duck. My siblings and mother do not share my interest in food, travel and hospitality – my father never travelled outside Australia.

Once I was a boy going to Church of England Sunday school and eating meat loaf. Now I am a Buddhist who meditates and eats Nepalese momo. When we retire, Joanne and I hope to spend six months a year in Thailand or the French countryside and six months a year here in

Australia. The changes in my tastes and attitude to food are also reflected in my tastes and attitude to life. And I am not merely a product of my family environment, I am also a product of the broader Australian society of the seventies, eighties and beyond, as well as multicultural Australia. Food was what helped change Australian society so dramatically. It is now a society that my grandfather old Wally would not recognise. I live a lifestyle that he never knew existed, nor could he have dreamt would one day exist – and all from food.

My advice would be to savour the moment; relish the good times and those special moments that you know will never happen again. Try all the food you can, avoid the food on the nose-to-tail list and wash it all down with a nice bottle of red. Life is too short to eat bad food.

Yes Chef!
Chef's Secrets ...

As soon as people find out I am a chef they always have a question to ask. How do I make restaurant quality mashed potato? How long does it take to cook pork belly? How can do you tell when the fish is done? Many of these questions are quite difficult to answer satisfactorily because I know the person asking is looking for exact answer, such as pork belly takes an hour to cook, fish takes six minutes, etc. But as a chef, much of the cooking I just do, without taking notice of exact details such as time or oven temperature. How long does it take to grill a portion of salmon? Answer: Until it's done. Same for the pork belly. What temperature should I have my oven on? Hot! Again it's not something I have ever paid much attention to. Do I have a recipe for garlic prawns? Well, no! I just cook them.

You would think after watching ten years of the rock star chefs on TV that all the questions have been answered. But people still feel we are holding back the real cooking tricks for ourselves and that chefs are like freemasons grand masters, mysterious and secretive. But the truth of the matter is that cooking itself is easy – getting 180 people to pay for your cooking every night, now that's the hard part.

When you prepare and cook a dish every day, after a very short period you just know when it's cooked – it's like a sixth sense. If you cook 50 steaks every day you soon get to know how long it takes to cook *that* meat on *that* grill at *that* temperature. It's very difficult to just say cook it for six minutes of each side. The variables are too great and I know full well that whomever I give advice to will take it literally, to the second.

In the kitchens I worked in ovens were always on full and flames were all burning flat out. In my day cooking was a sport, it wasn't gentle. Chefs were hard and cooking was fast and furious.

So how do I explain all that to a friend who wants to make garlic prawns just like he gets at his favorite restaurant? Even a simple dish has so many intricate components and timing variables that I just know there is a very good chance it won't work as well at home.

Chefs do need recipes for desserts and baked goods but the professional chef understands the cooking methods and in general has little need for recipes beyond a list of ingredients. Cooking is not about following directions and recipes: it's about understanding cooking methods, so please don't ask me for recipes because that's really hard for me to do. However, having made my excuses I will try to answer the questions I get asked the most.

Q: How do I make that really good mashed potatoes I get in restaurants?

A: There are three different ways.

Mashed potato 1: To get that really rich, smooth mashed potato you first need to boil the potatoes whole (use desiree potatoes), remove the skin, put the potatoes back on the stove to dry out just a little, then mash them and push through a sieve. Return to the stove and add little cream and a *lot* of butter, whipping the butter in with a fine whisk (ie up to about 40 per cent of the potato is butter).

Mashed potato 2: If you don't want to die of a heart attack replace the butter with a couple of tablespoons of good quality virgin olive oil. This will also give you a different flavour.

Mashed potato 3: You could also try making pomme duchess, the classical French potato dish. After boiling the potato, return to the stove to dry out a little. Then mash to very smooth with a small amount of butter and finish with egg yolk (about 3 per kilo potato). Pipe into small towers on a tray and bake in oven (secret ingredient: add a dash of nutmeg).

Q: How do I get nice crunchy roast potatoes?

A: Toss the potatoes in flour and seasoning first, and roast in duck fat or dripping for extra flavour. Cook in a separate pan to the meat. On Christmas day when you have 20 people over for lunch, deep fry the potato first to form a robust crust before putting in the oven to roast.

Q: What is an easy sauce I can make for my fish or steak?

A: Use flavoured butters, which can be easily prepared ahead of time. Mix soft butter with any ingredients you like, garlic, parsley, lemon, pepper, spice mixes, olives, anchovy, benito flakes, mustard, etc. Place in foil and roll out to a cylinder shape. These can be stored in the fridge or even frozen. To use, cut the butter in a disc, melt in the fish pan after cooking the fish and dribble the sauce over the fish. For meat dishes, place the disc of butter on top of the steak just before serving.

Q: What is something different I can serve with a roast?

A: Try roast vegetables balsamic. Cut assorted vegetables (potato, onion, sweet potato, carrot) into about 2 cm cubes. Add whole cloves of garlic (skin on), rosemary, salt, pepper and olive oil. Roast in hot oven and then five minutes before ready drizzle the vegetables in balsamic vinegar and return to oven for a few minutes.

Q: Why does my Asian food never work very well at home?

A: The big problem with cooking Asian food at home is the power of your stove. Wok cooking requires enormous gas flames that look and sound like a small jet engine. It is impossible to wok fry a family meal of four at home in one batch. Your flame is so small it cannot fry the food; it becomes boiled. To counteract this you must cook in small batches on a full blast flame and then add all together at the end for one final mix.

Q: My curries never taste right. What's the secret to a good curry?

A: One of the big mistakes home cooks make is not to cook the spices first. The spices need to be cooked in a little oil or ghee before adding any other ingredients.

Q: My poached eggs never work, how do I poach an egg?

A: Add a little vinegar to water for poaching eggs. This lowers the pH level and sets the egg white quicker, which holds it together better. Once the water has boiled, let it slow down to a very gentle simmer. Place the egg in a small ramekin first and then gently slip into the water.

Q: What's your secret Asian ingredient?

A: Shaoxing cooking wine, it costs about $2 a bottle but adds so much to any dish.

Q: How do I cook a crab or crayfish?

A: There are lots of different ways to cook shellfish but to poach or boil it we use what is called a *court bouillon*. In a pot of water add some carrot, celery, onion, parsley stalks, bay leaves, peppercorns, salt and lemon or white wine. Cook for about five minutes then add the seafood.

Q: How do I prevent a soufflé from falling?

A: You don't, it has to be served immediately. If it sits for a minute while waiting for a waiter you're in trouble (so is the waiter).

Q: How do I toss things in a pan the way I see chefs do on TV?

A: Get a small pan and put about three spoons of salt in the pan. Make the far end of your pan a little lower than your wrist and flick it up as you push the salt to the bottom of the pan. Do fifty times a day for two weeks and then you should be able to start on real food.

Q: Why do chefs drink so much?

A: Because we can.

Q: Why do chefs swear so much?

A: Commercial cooking is an intense situation and we like to emphasise the point.

Q: How can I improve my barbeque cooking?

A: Charcoal – don't eat it, use it for cooking. The flavour you can get from grilling a few steaks or some seafood on a simple charcoal barbeque in the backyard is not to be underestimated. Don't use gas or briquettes; it must be wooden charcoal.

Q: How do I make garlic prawns?

A: Sorry, no recipes!

Q: What's best for sautéing: butter or oil?

A: Using half butter, half oil gives you the best of both worlds. The richness of the butter combines beautifully with the robustness of the oil.

Q: How do I stop my rice from sticking together?

A: It's probably best to start with making a classical French pilaff; you can use a rice cooker if you like. The secret is to use long grain rice and wash it till the water becomes clear as it runs off; this washes away the starch. Add a small amount of sautéed onion and a little oil, coat the rice with the oil, then add a couple of whole garlic cloves, salt and a couple of bay leaves. Add stock (one part rice to one and a half parts stock), cook, then discard the garlic and bay leaves after cooking. Fold a little soft butter through the cooked rice with a gentle fork.

Q: Do I have to use real stock? Why is it so hard to make?

A: Yes. No it's not, so give it a go.

Q: Why is my pasta sloppy and lifeless?

A: You're overcooking it, most people do. As you are cooking take a bite of one strand and look closely at where you have bitten it. You are looking for that small section of uncooked pasta in the middle for the pasta to be al dente, or just a little bit firm. Serve then.

Q: Why are potato dishes on a menu always called 'pomme' when pomme means apple?

A: In French a potato is called *pomme de terre* which means apple of the earth. For convenience it gets shortened to pomme.

Q: What's a secret cheese platter ingredient that will make my friends go wow?

A: Use pickled cherries. Take large whole cherries and add to a small pot with red wine vinegar, a little sugar and a little water. Bring to boil and take off the heat to cool as soon as it comes to boil. Only cook a small amount at a time. Cool and serve with cheese of your choice. Mmmmm!

Q: How do I cook old-fashioned ox tongue?

A: Don't know, don't care!

Q: The white sauce (béchamel) for my lasagna is always lumpy. What am I doing wrong?

A: The white sauce is based on a roux (a mixture of butter and flour). When adding milk the rule is hot roux, cold milk or hot milk, cold roux. Adding hot milk to a hot roux will thicken and become lumpy before you have the chance to stir smooth. Make sure you use a whisk to beat the mixture, this will also help with any lumps.

Q: What temperature should my fridge be?

A: Below 5°C

Q: How do I peel and cut onions without crying?

A: Try to stand in a breeze near the exhaust fan, be fast and don't be such a sook. Suffering is good for your soul.

Q: My burger or meatloaf is often dry, how can I prevent this?

A: In mincemeat type dishes like burgers, meatloaf and meatballs, soak some old bread in milk, squeeze out excess milk and add to the meat mixture. This gives body and holds the moisture better.

Q: What's the chef's secret to making good crepes?

A: Make the batter and let it sit for 30 to 60 minutes before cooking. This lets the starch molecules absorb the moisture and allows the gluten to relax.

Q: How is consommé made?

A: Okay, stop right there, now we are moving into dangerous territory that I may be kicked out of the chefs' club for!

Acknowledgements

I would like to acknowledge and thank the many people who made this book possible. Those who listened to me rave on for two years and those who pulled me back into line with some harsh truth.

First of all I would like to thank my wife Joanne for not making fun of me and for listening to every detail over and over again.

I would like to thank Samantha, Rex and the team at Finch Publishing for seeing the book behind the raw manuscript and having faith in the story, for holding my hand and guiding me in the clash of culture between the world of the kitchen and the world of publishing.

I would also like to thank my friends who read and gave honest opinions about the manuscript that enabled me to refine how I said what I wanted to say. In particular Joanne Fisher for her patience and advice and Stephen Ellis for telling me I swear too much.

I thank the team at Writers Victoria who support, educate and encourage emerging writers and provided a valuable manuscript assessment service that encouraged me to turn a rough collection of thoughts into a full blown memoir with a distinctly Australian voice. This book would not have been attempted without Anthony Bourdain having broken the ground before me and showing the world that the story of a working class chef was a worthwhile subject, and that a chef was capable of writing such a story.

Finally I would like to thank all those who over the years who have taught me to be me (in no particular order). My father Norm, my mother Moira, Gary, Andrea, Michael Donnelly, John F Kennedy, His Holiness the Dalai Lama, Robert F Kennedy, John Macdonald, Stephen Carter, Muhammad Ali, Aliesha, Tiarne, all the chefs that I ever cooked with, Stephen Tryon, Scott Merrick, the bull, Ped, the crew of the Tavern, the crew of Apollo 11, Buddha, Dianna and Mark.

Other Finch titles

Marzipan & Magnolias
Elizabeth Lancaster
ISBN: 9781921462207

No Chopsticks Required
Katrina Beikoff
ISBN: 9781921462290

When the Bough Breaks
Joanne W Jones
ISBN: 9781921462221

Catch Up With the Sun
Heidi Douglas
ISBN: 9781921462368

My Life in a Pea Soup
Lisa Nops
ISBN: 9781921462320

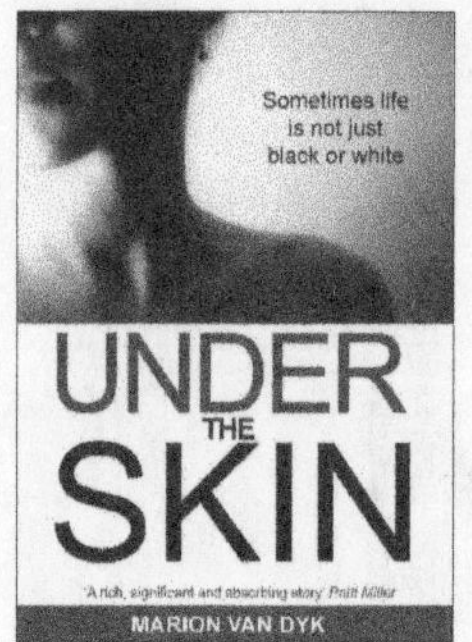

Under the Skin
Marion van Dyk
ISBN: 9781921462802